Divorce-Proof Man

DIVORCE-PROOF MAN

NINE LAWS
TO OWN YOUR ROLE,
WIN BACK HER RESPECT,
AND UNLOCK LASTING LOVE

MATT ENNS, MBA

NINE TRIES PUBLISHING

First Published in America and the U.K. by Nine Tries Publishing

First Published in Paperback, 2025

© Matt Enns, 2025

The right of Matt Enns to be identified as the Author of the work has been asserted by him in accordance with the Copyright, Designs and Patents Act 1988.

All rights reserved. The moral right of the author has been asserted.

Paperback ISBN 978-1-0686600-9-2

Edited, Formatted, and Published by Nine Tries Ltd, Saffron Walden, United Kingdom.

ninetries.co.uk

This book is dedicated to Whitney,
my storm, my inspiration, and the love of my life.

CONTENTS

1. It's Not Over — 7
2. The First Law — 15
3. The Second Law — 27
4. The Third Law — 41
5. The Fourth + Fifth Law — 54
6. The Sixth Law — 72
7. The Seventh Law — 87
8. The Eighth Law — 105
9. The Ninth Law — 126
10. Conclusion — 148
11. Want More Support? — 155
12. Appendix I: More Exercises — 156
13. Appendix II: More Notes — 165

"When a man finds victory over himself,
he finds a victory that no person can take away,
and every person can share."
– Thomas Merton

IT'S NOT OVER

I am very lucky to know some of the world's foremost authorities in the relationship space. These include best-selling authors, renowned speakers, and popular podcast hosts. I also count among some of my closest friends various psychologists, psychiatrists, and therapists. But as much as we all agree about the importance of people having healthy, vibrant relationships, I disagree with almost all of them about the core issue of relationship work—namely, when to leave.

Most experts will tell you that if your partner is not willing to work with you to heal the relationship, it's time to leave and find someone who actually wants to be with you. Of course, this is easy to understand. After all, we all deserve (and I certainly agree here) a spouse who 1) loves and values us, and 2) is willing to fight to make the relationship work. Any marriage that goes the distance will pass through phases that require real work from both partners in order to survive.

So where do I differ from my colleagues?

I don't believe a marriage is doomed if your wife isn't committed to making it work. I don't think that a marriage is destined to fail even if, right now, your wife is "done." If her mind is made up that it's "over." That although she loves you, she is no longer "in love with you." It doesn't even matter if she's told you that "it's always been bad," "we were never compatible," or "we have never had a sexual connection." I don't consider a marriage to be beyond repair just because your wife says she's unwilling to change, and never will be. As shocking as it might sound, I don't even think that it's too late when she proves by both word and deed that she's absolutely unwilling to do anything at all to even try to save the marriage.

So, why do I believe something that sounds so ridiculous? It's because seeing is believing—and in my work as a divorce-prevention expert, I've seen thousands of 'unsavable' relationships heal and flourish. Most of these marriages are now better than they'd ever been and the men inside them feel proud, fulfilled, and respected. To show you what I get to see on a regular basis, here are a few recent examples from our coaching at Sovereign Man.

The first example is about one of my clients who came home to a note from his wife explaining that she had felt dead in the relationship for years, that she knew he was the wrong man since their engagement, and that she'd never felt happy during their 11 years of marriage together. The note included a P.S. explaining that by the time he read this, she would already be on a flight across the Atlantic Ocean, leaving their home in Europe to start again in South America. To make things even harder for him, she also let him know that she'd changed her phone number, blocked his email and social media accounts, and that if he wanted to communicate with her, he could do so by emailing her cousin. That and she stipulated he could only email her cousin in regard to the divorce papers he should expect to receive within the month.

10 weeks after he and I started working together, they were on vacation together in Bali to renew their vows. Six months after this, she could not stop bragging to her friends about her amazing husband and the "marriage of her dreams."

The second example comes from a client married to a feminist professor at a local college. He became dismayed when his wife decided that marriage was inherently destructive to her mental health and she was destined for unhappiness as long as she was with him. She informed him that their marriage would henceforth exist solely for their two kids, with plans to divorce him once the youngest left home in about 8 years. She added that he could divorce her sooner if he chose, but otherwise, they'd remain co-parents—never intimate—and she'd refuse any alternative under any circumstances. She considered this rather generous and vowed that she wouldn't go to therapy or discuss the matter any further, let alone try to work on their marriage together.

Two weeks after he joined my program she initiated sex with him for the first time since the birth of their youngest child, more than six years earlier. Within the first month, she actually cooked him dinner—something she had *never done once* and believed to be inherently demeaning for a wife to do. Within a few months, she was radically committed to their marriage and he was himself experiencing happiness for the first time in many years. The last I heard, about five months after our first session, she was bringing a home-cooked lunch to his office three days a week—and if that wasn't enough, they'd snuck down to their car in the back parking lot for some "alone time" more than once.

I could list a hundred other stories like this, but what ties them all together is that the wife did not want the marriage to succeed and wasn't willing to try to save it, and I only worked with the husband. In the stories that I just shared with you, I never met or spoke with either wife. The same goes for almost every other client I see. The work that we do together is husband-focused. It's about changing the man and that, in the end, is what changes the marriage.

What many relationship experts miss about these situations is that when the man changes in the relationship—when he shows up in a new way—the woman tends to change in response. This is the deeper meaning of *leadership* in a marriage. An improved man is an improved marriage—and married women can feel the difference. They sense when something shifts and, eventually, they shift with it. But that's not the message you hear from most experts. Indeed, both they and society grossly underestimate the power that a man has to change his circumstances when he takes radical ownership of his marriage and his own behavior.

I learned this lesson the hard way. Let me explain by taking you back to before I worked as a men's coach. Back to when my wife, Whitney, and I began dating. We were just twenty-three years old at the time. I was pursuing a career in finance and earning an MBA on the side, but beneath the surface my life was a mess. Already a severe alcoholic, I also suffered from massive social anxiety and had significant issues with anger, dishonesty and hurting those I cared about. Whitney was irresponsible in her own ways as well. She did not take life seriously, instead doing whatever felt like fun. For many years, this had meant jumping from job to job, and even country to country, trying to escape her pain and any other problems that arose. But dating each other was a genuine bright spot for both of us—until, at twenty-four, we got pregnant. We decided to do the 'right thing' and had a shotgun wedding, but the odds of having a successful marriage were not high.

In fact, after seven years of non-stop fights, resentment, anger and hopelessness—plus another kid—we very nearly got divorced. Indeed, we separated and I lived alone in an AirBnB, missing my children, but "knowing" that my marriage simply could not be saved. Sure, I missed Whitney terribly, and it broke my heart to only see my kids every other week, but we were "not compatible" and it was "better for the kids" to not see us fighting—and just like that, I believed everything the therapists had told us.

Though we ended up living separately for six (very painful) months, this experience taught me some valuable things. It helped that by this point in my own journey I'd spent the past few years going through hundreds of books, lectures, and podcasts about my own pain, anxiety, addictions and regret. I'd always been a voracious learner, but now I was steeped in Jungian psychology, existential therapy, masculine archetypal frameworks, neuro-linguistic programming, mystical religious practices, and so much more. This had given me a new lens to view the world and I decided to apply it not just to myself but to my marriage.

This led me to ask myself two questions about my marriage: "What am I hiding from myself that I really don't want to admit?" and "what can I actually control?" The answer to the first question was very painful. I had a lot of short-comings as a husband which I had either ignored, minimized, or blamed on Whitney. I'd made her into the bad guy for being unappreciative, unhelpful and unhealthy. Don't get me wrong, many of my gripes about Whitney were entirely warranted at the time, but I began to understand that my behavior as a husband contributed to all of them. I started to see that she was not the *only* problem and that, in fact, I was a much bigger problem that I was ever willing to admit. The answer to the second question was, as it always is, "me." I can control my thoughts, my emotions, and my behavior. That's it.

So, I spent some time dissecting our relationship through this lens. Then I asked myself, what if, instead of fighting with Whitney, blaming her, and making her responsible for all the struggles in our marriage… I owned my role. Fully and completely. How might the situation change if I showed up as the man I could be, *the man I was meant to be?* In short, what if instead of trying to change her, I changed me?

Getting Whitney to meet with me wasn't an easy sell, but when we finally sat down together—after six months apart, only communicating with each other about finances and the kids—I told her that I understood why she had disconnected. That I got why she was so unhappy. That I could see why she couldn't bear to continue in the marriage. I told her that I didn't blame her. I admitted that I had work to do.

Whitney was completely shocked by this. Both the sincerity and the accuracy of my insights about her pain caused her to doubt the path of divorce just enough to open the door. She wasn't going to move back in: but she would hear me out and consider working on it. But, a week later, amazed at what she had been seeing, she broke her lease and moved back in with me—just like the wives of so many of my clients have done since.

That's not to say it was smooth sailing from then on. The next year was not easy, but I did my best to own my role. I engaged with her from a position of non-judgment, and as a result I began to understand her and how radically different her mind and her emotions were from mine. I began to apply my insane appetite for learning to figuring out just how different she was from me. What I discovered blew my mind. I began to understand something that nobody taught me, that nobody in my generation was taught: the different roles that men and women need to play in a relationship. I'm not talking just about who cooks the dinner or goes to work or anything like that. I'm talking about the different roles men and women have when it comes to connection, safety, and disagreements in a relationship.

For example, I learned that my wife wasn't fundamentally unappreciative, selfish, or crazy. Rather, the problematic stuff she'd been sending my way was a direct response to her feeling unloved and unsafe. The fact that feeling unsafe could manifest in such 'crazy' behavior had never crossed my mind as a man, but her concern for safety permeated every aspect of her being—and our marriage—in ways I could never previously have fathomed. This was a wake-up call to say the least.

There were other lessons too. I came to realize that our fights—which I'd previously thought were arguments over facts—were more often than not her needing to feel the strength of my love and to experience my immovability in the face of her own emotional turmoil. So, too, I learned that despite the fundamental differences between male and female communication—differences that can seem so staggering it's a marvel anyone stays married at all—bridging that communication divide is quite straightforward when you have the right tools and understanding.

But what I learned more than anything was that when I changed, she changed in response. There was always a delay—sometimes it was only minutes, but sometimes it was many months—but inevitably the positive changes that I was making resulted in positive changes in her as well. This all happened without her going to therapy, without her reading some relationship book, without her *really even trying*, and often without her even noticing that she had changed.

From this profound transformation in both of us, I began to see what leadership might actually mean for a man in the context of his marriage. It wasn't like that of a CEO or a dictator, but there was something powerful about it—like that of a king transforming his own kingdom. A king that sought to improve himself above all else… and ended up improving his whole kingdom as well. Often in ways he couldn't have imagined.

Truth be told, when I first sat down with Whitney to convince her to give us another shot, I was really just aiming at a decent marriage. At the time, I believed that was about as good as it could get for us—and that's also what I saw in most of the marriages around me. I didn't even really know what a great marriage would look like, and I definitely thought that would not happen for us. But after a year back together we were not just decent... we were amazing. She was far more 'the dream wife' than I'd ever dared imagine, and she could not stop telling me what an amazing husband I was. In the deepest sense of the word, we were... happy. And we still are, massively. It's been years, but even now as I type this, I am filled with genuine awe at the level of joy that my marriage brings me every day.

I'm telling you this not because I want to make you envious. It's because I want to make you excited. I want to get your hopes up. I truly believe that what happened for me—and for the countless men I've coached—can happen for you too. That's why I left my career in finance, even though I was succeeding in a big way at one of the world's largest wealth management firms. In fact, I was lined-up to be making seven-figures a year by the time I was forty—but I sold my financial practice, left Canada, and moved with my family to Texas in order to found Sovereign Man. We did this without a second thought because we knew that what I'd learned was too important, too meaningful, and too necessary to keep it to myself. There were men who needed to hear this. Men like you.

Since then, Sovereign Man has flourished. I've had the privilege of personally working with hundreds of men who have saved their marriages from the brink of divorce. I've likewise received thousands of messages from men telling me that my teachings have resulted in their marriages healing and becoming divorce-proof. It has been a long, wild, painful, exciting, and deeply meaningful journey. A journey I thank God for every day.

This book, and the Nine Laws it contains, is a roadmap for helping you make a similar journey. It is my deepest hope and my firm belief that it will help you to get to where you need to go. To become the man your marriage needs you to be. To become the man you are *meant* to be.

Notes to Self

THE FIRST LAW: MASTER YOURSELF

Return Of The King

America needs more kings. Not literal ones. George III was quite enough. But metaphorically, we need more men to be the kings of their own kingdoms. To be leaders in their own lives. Men who have taken responsibility for themselves, their marriages, their families and more. Adding to the social, cultural, and moral capital of this country, and like a rising tide, they lift all ships. This isn't just a nostalgic wish for some bygone era of chivalry or crowns—it's a desperate call for men to step into their power, to claim the authority they've let slip through their fingers. Because right now, too many of us are drifting, lost in a sea of distractions and dependencies, while the world around us crumbles under the weight of chaos. We need men who can stand tall, shining like a lighthouse amidst the storm; men who can rebuild what's been broken—not just for themselves, but for everyone who depends on them.

Think about the state of things: families fracturing, communities unravelling, values eroding like sandcastles against the waves. It's not hard to see why. When men stop leading their own lives, when they let lesser forces take the reins, the ripple effects spread far beyond their front doors. A man who's mastered himself doesn't just save his marriage—he strengthens his family, his neighborhood, his workplace, his nation. He becomes a pillar, a lighthouse, a force for good in a world that's starving for direction. That's the kind of king I'm talking about: not a tyrant with a sword, but a strong, free, and loving man with a spine of steel and a wide-open heart.

I deeply believe this is the only solution to the unprecedented—and often insane—cultural, economic, and relational crises that we are facing as a society. We're drowning in noise—political shouting matches, economic roller coasters, and a culture that celebrates weakness over strength. Relationships are buckling under the strain of it all, with divorce rates climbing and trust evaporating like morning dew. The old fixes don't work anymore; throwing money or therapy at the problem won't cut it. What we need is a revolution from within, a return to men owning their lives with clarity and conviction. Because when a man rises to his potential, when he takes the helm of his own soul, everything else starts to fall into place. It's not a quick fix—it's a slow, steady climb—but it's the only path that leads us out of this mess.

It's what we need, but it's probably not where you are. You may want to be a King, but your life seems stuck in *slave-mode*. In this state, you're being held back from becoming the leading authority in your life. This might take the form of something really obvious, like an addiction to drugs, pornography, or something else. Maybe it's the bottle you reach for after a long day, promising relief but delivering chains. Maybe it's the screen that pulls you in with its endless scroll of escape, numbing you to the reality you're avoiding. Or maybe it's a quieter vice, like gambling away a little too much of your pay check or chasing highs that leave you lower than before. These are shackles you can see, feel, and name—and they're heavy.

It could be that you're a slave to your wife—her approval or her making you feel loved—either of which can result in fits of anxiety and long stretches of panic. Maybe you're tiptoeing around her moods, second-guessing every word, desperate for a smile or a kind word to tell you you're enough. Or maybe you're tethered to her affection, measuring your worth by how she looks at you, spiraling when it's not there. That's a prison too, one built of emotional bars, and it keeps you small, reactive, always waiting for someone else to set you free.

But you could just as easily be a slave to yourself—your need for space or freedom, which makes you especially avoidant when things become harder at home. You feel the tension rising, the arguments brewing, and instead of facing it head-on, you retreat. You check out, physically or mentally, chasing solitude like it's a lifeline. You tell yourself you're just "taking a break," but deep down, you know it's cowardice dressed up as independence. That need for escape becomes your master, pulling you away from the life you're meant to lead.

Sadly, the list goes on. Maybe you're chained to your lower impulses. Hunger calls, and you let it rule. You're raiding the fridge at midnight, not because you're starving, but because boredom or stress told you to. Lust whispers, and you obey without thought. It's not just the obvious temptations—it's the fleeting glances, the fantasies, the quick surrenders that chip away at your integrity. Laziness wraps its arms around you, convincing you to stay where you are and that's exactly what you do. You sink into the couch, the bed, the routine, letting inertia dictate your days while opportunities pass you by. But it could just as easily be issues with anger, immaturity, and greed—you are a victim of the tyranny of your own emotions. Anger flares up, and you lash out, leaving wreckage in your wake. Immaturity keeps you stuck in boyhood, dodging responsibility like it's a game. Greed whispers promises of more, driving you to chase shadows instead of building something real.

Whatever it is, the effect is the same. These are moments where you cede your *sovereignty* to something else. This is when the king within you steps down, handing over the crown to something lesser. It's not a dramatic abdication with trumpets and tears—it's quiet, insidious, a slow leak of power you barely notice until it's gone. Every time you give in, you're not just losing a battle; you're handing over your throne to a usurper who doesn't care about your kingdom. And the longer you let it happen, the harder it is to take it back.

Think about that for a second. Every time you let those emotional impulses take over, you're surrendering. You're abdicating the throne of your own life to forces that don't have your best interests at heart. That's not just a bad day; that's a pattern, a system you're stuck in. And as long as that system runs the show, you'll never act from your Sovereign Self—the version of you that's strong, steady, and confident. And until you begin the hard work of mastering yourself, you won't be able to master the art of marriage. It's a brutal truth: your wife can't thrive under a king who's bowing to shadows. Your family can't flourish when its leader is a slave. You've got to break free—not just for you, but for them.

Two Paths

You're probably familiar with Robert Frost's famous poem, 'The Road Not Taken'. In it, the narrator is walking through the woods only to discover that the path he's following divides in two. Forced to choose between them, he opts for the "road less traveled." It's a very good poem, but for our purposes, it's incomplete life advice. Frost's narrator gets to pick one path and muse about the other—nice and tidy, a poetic little moment. But life isn't a stroll through the woods with a single fork. It's messier, tougher, and it demands more. In this book, you must walk both roads: one path is toward self-improvement, going from Slave to Sovereign; the second is improving your marriage, nurturing it from weakness to strength. You don't get to choose one and call it a day—you've got to tackle both, because they're inseparable, like a fire and its fuel.

Let's break it down. The marriage path starts with understanding—really seeing your wife, not just as a partner or a problem, but as a person with her own wiring, her own fears, her own language of love and pain. Healing the relationship begins with understanding who your partner is and how she operates. Maybe she shuts down when you raise your voice because it echoes something from her past. Maybe she needs words you've never thought to give, or silence you've never offered. From that education comes communication: the process of conveying that you get her and that you get it. That it's no longer a mystery to you why you're disconnected. It's saying, "I see you, I hear you, and I'm here," in a way she can feel, not just hear. And after that comes the rewarding work of reconnecting and rebuilding her sense of safety with you, earning her trust, and reviving lost intimacy. It's showing up, day after day, proving you're not the man who checked out or blew up—it's laying bricks for a bridge she can finally cross back to you.

The other path, by contrast, is not about her; it's about you. It's personal, self-improvement work and it's imperative that you do it. Not only because you won't be able to implement the lessons on the relationship side if you haven't changed as a man—she will recognize there hasn't been a change—but also because you need to be a bigger man. You need to be a better man. The world needs the very best version of you. You should not be living a life where you are a slave to your lower impulses, where you are a slave to your past traumas, where you are a slave to your emotions, allowing such things to get the best of you. All of that needs to be addressed for the King and his Kingdom to truly heal. For that reason, at the end of every chapter there's a section dedicated to doing your personal work. This will include guidance for reflection, breathwork, and journaling. Do these, and you will see substantial results. Don't... and you won't.

This self-path is about excavation—digging into the muck of your own soul to find what's holding you back. Maybe it's a wound from childhood, a father's harsh words still echoing in your head, telling you you'll never measure up. Maybe it's a betrayal from a friend that left you guarded, unwilling to trust even the woman you swore to love. Or maybe it's just the weight of years spent coasting, letting life happen to you instead of shaping it. Whatever it is, you've got to face it. You've got to name it, wrestle with it, and put it in its place. Because if you don't, it'll keep pulling the strings, and you'll stay a puppet instead of a king.

The Once And Future King

To go from slave to Sovereign, you must crown your inner-king. This begins with imagining a Sovereign Self that sits inside you—a better, smarter, more powerful version of you—one that is always at the helm, quietly steering the ship. This isn't some mythical figure; it's you, with a straighter back and clearer eyes. It's you, actively thinking your way through situations, rather than passively responding to them. It's you, practicing virtues rather than prolonging vices. The more you lean into this version of yourself, the more it becomes second nature. You'll stumble at first, like a child learning to walk, but with time, this place of sovereignty will become your default. As a man, you'll finally grow into your full masculinity.

This isn't fantasy—it's a blueprint. That Sovereign Self isn't a stranger; it's the man you were born to be, buried under layers of habit and hurt. Picture him, clearly in your mind, right now: shoulders squared, gaze steady, voice calm but firm. He doesn't flinch when the Storm hits—he navigates it. He doesn't crumble under criticism—he learns from it. He's not perfect, but he's disciplined, deliberate, and driven by something bigger than fleeting urges. Every time you choose him over the slave, you're forging that crown, tempering it in the fire of your own resolve.

Men often enter my programs at their lowest: anxious, passive, angry, weak, shackled by the need for approval. But after just a little while, something remarkable happens. They radiate a quiet confidence. Their wives, their children, even their co-workers sense the shift. Strangers approach them for advice. This is what happens when you awaken the King within, that sovereign energy tied to the divine. For some, this connection comes through Christianity. For others, it's another faith or simply the whisper of a higher purpose. But the principle holds: activate the King, and the Kingdom begins to heal. I've seen it play out in real time—men who couldn't look me in the eye on day one walking out six weeks later like they own the room. Their wives notice first: a softer tone, a firmer boundary, a presence that wasn't there before. It's not magic; it's mastery.

When you carry this King energy, it's impossible to hide. Humans are wired to pick up on the smallest signals—body language, posture, the tilt of a chin. Your energy speaks before you do. Mythology has known this truth for centuries. Look at the stories: when the King is right, the land flourishes. When the King is corrupt or absent, the world falls apart. *The Lion King* nailed it: Scar takes the throne, and everything withers; Simba returns, and the earth sings again. Shakespeare does the same in *Macbeth*. That's because these aren't just fairy tales, they are narrative articulations of a deeper truth. When you're aligned with your higher self, your family feels it. Your wife feels it (even from the other room… with the door shut and the light turned off). Even your dog feels it. And until you reach this place, no amount of relationship advice will stick. Advice that is practiced from a place of insecurity feels hollow; your wife, intuitive as she is, will see straight through it. She's not looking for words—she's looking for you, the real you, the King she married or hoped you'd become.

As should be clear to you by now, transformation takes work. There's no shortcut, no easy hack. That's why this book is designed as a sequence: every chapter is followed by instructions for doing reflective work. Many of the sovereignty exercises can be found in Appendix I. There are likewise some lined blank pages you can takes notes on in Appendix II. Other exercises are included at the end of each chapter, along with guided meditations, journaling prompts, and breathwork activities. Taken together, these all build toward something bigger. Some of it will feel silly. You'll want to skip steps. Don't. Each exercise lays a foundation for the next. This isn't just about creating a deeper connection with your wife (though that's part of it). It's about finding your purpose, leaning into your unique strengths, and striving for something far more meaningful than either wealth or status. It's about waking up every day knowing who you are and why you're here—not just for her, but for you, for the man you're meant to be.

Heads Up

The work ahead is not for the fainthearted. The circumstances you're living in—whether they're wreckage you've caused, Storms you've stumbled into, or the slow rot of neglect—will ask more of you than you think you can give. And then they'll ask for more. The pay-off is a life of personal and marital satisfaction. The reward is to feel joy once again. To feel your Inner Power. It's to fire on all cylinders. To get back to your A-game. But getting there can be a draining process. Emotionally. Mentally. Spiritually. You'll be forced to relearn things you should've known and unlearn things you thought you couldn't live without. The habits, the knee-jerk reactions, the warped ways of thinking that brought you here? They've got to go. And that will hurt. You'll feel pain—raw and sharp, or maybe dull and grinding—that you thought you'd left behind. Or worse, pain you swore you'd never let yourself feel again. But here it is. And here you are. So, what are you going to do?

This isn't a weekend seminar or a feel-good pep talk—it's a gauntlet. You might be staring at the ruins of a fight you started, the silence of a wife you've pushed away, or the creeping decay of years spent drifting. That's your starting line, not your finish. And it's going to demand everything: every ounce of grit, every shred of honesty, every drop of faith you can muster. You'll face moments where you want to quit, where the old slave whispers that it's easier to stay down. But the King in you knows better—he knows the prize is worth the fight.

To get the most out of this book, you're going to need to create space—for yourself. That means carving out time in the morning and again in the evening. Not hours, but enough to be still. To think. To work through the exercises. To reflect on who you are—and who you're becoming. The self-work in these pages is just a starting point. If you want to go deeper, move faster, and see real transformation, consider joining one of our Sovereign Man coaching programs or diving into the full coursework. You can find those on our website. That level of support can change everything.

But don't stop there. Get back into your body. Go to the gym. Break a sweat. It matters. So does eating well, getting some sunlight, going on walks, waking up early. These aren't side quests—they're signals to yourself that you're rising

Still, the two most important things you need—more than any program or protocol—are *hope* and *courage*. Hope that you're not stuck like this forever. And courage to act like that's true. If you have those two things, you can change your life. And trust me, the sacrifice is worth the reward.

Think of it like this: every morning you carve out, every rep you push through, every journal entry you scratch out—it's a brick in the wall of your new kingdom. You're not just killing time; you're building a legacy. The gym isn't about vanity—it's about waking up your body so your mind can follow. The coaching isn't a luxury—it's a forge where your resolve gets hammered into shape. And hope and courage? They're the fuel and the fire. You've got to believe this can work, and you've got to step into the ring every damn day to make it happen. Because when you do, when you finally stand as that King, everything changes—your marriage, your life, your world.

Long live the King!

A Man's Work

You've reached the end of the chapter on the first law, which means you've got work to do. These four exercises aren't theory—they're your initiation. Do them with honesty, hunger, and humility. Carve out the time. Face yourself. The King in you is waiting on the other side of effort. Don't just read them—actually DO them. Begin building your inner throne.

1) Your Version of Heaven and Hell

Instructions: Find a quiet space and take 15–20 minutes with your notebook. Write two vivid scenes, and write them in a way where it would be entertaining for someone else to read. First, imagine life five years from now if your inner slave—fear, vice, or avoidance—controls you. What's your mindset, your marriage, your day-to-day? Be raw and honest. Then, picture five years with the King in charge—strong, purposeful, loving leadership. How do you speak, move, love? Feel the strength in your posture. This isn't a fantasy—it's your map. Revisit weekly to stay hungry for Heaven and properly afraid to Hell.

Purpose: This exercise creates a push-pull force in your subconscious mind to reject a wasted life and pursue sovereignty, setting the tone for your future transformation. It begins the process of aligning your default reactions with a future you've purposefully chosen.

2) Shadow Inventory

Instructions: You can't defeat what you won't name. Spend 20 minutes listing 5–10 traits you hide or hate—like anger, insecurity, a chameleon-like mask you wear. For each, note a moment it surfaced and how it hurt you or your marriage. Then, write one way to turn that flaw into strength (e.g., insecurity into vulnerability). This isn't about shame—it's about forging a crown from your flaws. Keep it private, and revisit to track growth.

Purpose: This inventory confronts self-sabotaging patterns, helping you to master yourself.

3) Core Values

Instructions: A king lives by a code—define yours. Take 15–20 minutes to write down a list of values (things like honesty, courage, wisdom), and select three that you want to live by—perhaps even you'd die for. For your chosen three, note what it means to you and a moment you lived it. Think of these as the pillars of your kingdom. Revisit them monthly to stay aligned. Feel free to Google a list of values to help you select yours.

Purpose: This establishes guiding principles for your sovereignty.

4) Breathwork (4-7-8 Method)

Instructions: Kings don't fold under pressure—they take a deep breath. Practise by standing tall in a quiet spot. Inhale for 4 seconds, hold for 7, exhale for 8. Do 4–8 rounds daily, especially when temptations hit—booze, porn, anger. Feel your body steady, your mind clear. Learn to rule your body and your nervous system with wisdom.

Purpose: This builds emotional and physical regulation, a foundational skill for sovereignty.

Notes to Self

THE SECOND LAW: BE THE LIGHTHOUSE

Lighthouse Wanted

Frank Sinatra famously sang that love and marriage go together like a horse and carriage. He could just as well have said that love and marriage go together like a Lighthouse and a Storm. It's certainly more appropriate.

Every marriage faces Storms, not least because some people are stormier than others. You're probably married to one, and I can say this with confidence because *most* women Storm at their husbands when they feel emotionally overwhelmed. In these situations, your wife may hurl whatever she is feeling at you—namely her fears and insecurities. She might slam you with what seems like unfair accusations or inaccurate facts. But as all men must learn, this is not actually her speaking. It is her *Storm* speaking. It is not a genuine representation of how she truly feels about you. Rather, it's a wife's way of searching for her husband's strength. It's her femininity stress-testing your masculinity, because she needs to know that whatever's overwhelming her isn't going to overwhelm you. In these situations, the Lighthouse should keep *shining its stable, loving light*—illuminating her darkness with courage, care, and curiosity. Do that, and the Storm will pass. Be strong, and your wife will discover her own strength. Rise to the occasion, and your marriage will rise with it.

But as we've already established, marriages don't improve unless the man improves. That's not because men are to blame for everything that's broken. It's because men have the right and the responsibility to change themselves. That's it. Your power only extends as far as your person. You've probably tried at some point to change your wife—and maybe you did… but more likely that change was not to your benefit. Instead, remember that *positive change begins with you*. It starts with understanding who you are as a husband and who your wife is as a woman. It starts with coming to grips with the Lighthouse and the Storm. So, let's begin.

Being The Lighthouse

Being the Lighthouse is the single greatest gift the masculine can offer the feminine. But it's a gift that you'll need to keep on giving, because emotional Storms can reoccur frequently—especially during the recovery phase of a struggling marriage. This isn't a weakness, but it is a difference. How you handle this difference will define your marriage.

The reasons for an emotional Storm can be many. On the one hand, you may have done something that's made her feel disconnected or unsafe. On the other, the Storm might have absolutely nothing to do with you—it's just the weight of life pressing down on her, or there's something she's struggling to make sense of. Whatever the reason, the Storm is coming your way.

It's important not to misunderstand the Storm. When it's raging at you—when outbursts abound and accusations fly or unfair 'facts' get thrown at you—the Storm can feel aggressive, like it wants to knock you over. But what the Storm is actually doing is Testing you. She's looking for your weaknesses, not so she can knock you over—but to make sure that you can handle it. Handle *her*. To make sure that you're strong enough to be relied upon when life's various Storms inevitably come your way.

In time, we'll cover how you can handle the details—how to respond when she throws hurtful stuff at you and how you can engage with the specifics of your own situation. But for now, there's just one thing you need to understand: what she's really looking for is for you to stand above the Storm. She's not asking for you to solve it, to argue with it, or to get pulled into it. She's asking you to be *bigger* than the Storm—to be unaffected by her fears when everything else feels like it's slipping away.

To do this, it helps to understand that Storms can happen for multiple reasons. The first is because a woman wants to know if what she's feeling is really as bad as it seems. It's almost like she's doing market research, testing out her own panic on a focus group. Do you feel the same way she does? Does the stress from her own life—her work, friends, and family—have the same impact on you as it does on her? When she shares it, do you get emotionally riled up too? If so, she'll think that she's right to be concerned. Maybe it is *every bit as bad as she feels it is*. After all, even her protector seems destabilized by it. If not, maybe she's got it wrong. Maybe it's not so bad. After all, her husband really, genuinely, doesn't seem fazed by it. Maybe she can be calm too. But whichever way it goes, remember that you are your wife's *most important* reference point during the Storm.

Unfortunately, rather than standing tall in the Storm, most men get lost in it. They hear their wife say something that's factually wrong, unfair, or even insulting—and they get defensive. They take the bait. Because they feel hurt, they say or do something hurtful in return. *They Storm back.* The problem with this is that it confirms to her that *it must be just as bad—or even worse!*—than she imagined. Just look how emotional it's making *him.* And, apart from making the Storm bigger, it's entirely unnecessary. It doesn't have to go this way. It's only happening because either the man has misunderstood why his wife is Storming, or he's failed to Storm-proof himself in the first place. If it's the latter, it means he hasn't done the internal work necessary to stand firm in himself. He's a man… but he hasn't learned how to really be masculine. The result is that before he knows it, he's getting blown around by the Storm too. Now both people are Storm-tossed, stuck in a swirling mess of emotions. It doesn't take a genius to know that nothing good will come from this.

When a woman Storms, what she really needs you to do is to remain *calm, caring, and curious.* She doesn't want you to bow before the Storm *or* to run away from it. This just means the Storm is now the most powerful force in your household. What she really needs is for you to be her Lighthouse. To be upright and strong, unshaken in the wind, not tipping over—just spinning your light, steady and constant, guiding her towards safety. Showing her, through your stability, that *it's not actually that bad*. That's what she's looking for. That's *your job, your gift*. Remember this: she will read way more into your emotional state during her Storm than she will into whatever you say (in fact, what you say might not even register at all).

It doesn't matter who wins the argument. It doesn't matter who was right. In fact, you can probably recall occasions where you 'won' the factual battle but lost the emotional war, because the fallout from that fight left both of you feeling more disconnected than before. In much the same way, there'll be times she 'won,' but it didn't make her happy. That's because *she doesn't care about winning like you do*. What she wants is to feel that you're *bigger* than the Storm, that you're *bigger* than whatever this is, that you're *bigger* than her chaos.

When she's Storming, what she's feeling is: "this is too much. It's overwhelming me." She's afraid, deep down, that maybe it's all as bad as she thinks. Maybe the world *really is* going to end! But if she throws that Storm at you, if she unleashes all those emotions, and you don't flinch—if you don't sway, if you don't get destabilized—then a shift happens inside of her. She begins to think "Okay, maybe it's not as bad as I feared. Maybe I'm not drowning. He's still here. He seems OK. Maybe I can calm down. Maybe I can be safe."

This brings us to the heart of the matter. Or rather, the center of the Storm. You're not supposed to 'fix' the Storm. Your purpose isn't to prove her wrong. Your mission is to remain *stable*. To show her through your own courage, care, and curiosity that she's not alone, that what's overwhelming for her isn't going to overwhelm you. That you are her place of safety. And when she sees you standing steady, untoppled by the Storm, she will eventually… relax. She can soften and stare up at you with Bambi eyes. Because she now knows she can *lean on you*—because you are bigger than the Storm.

Case in Point

Let's imagine this dynamic in a different way. Imagine a little girl at the park who falls and scrapes her knee. She runs over to her dad, tears in her eyes, asking, "Daddy, is it bad? Is it bleeding? Do I need a doctor?" She's spiraling downward, overwhelmed by her worst fears. Her dad looks at her calmly and says, "Honey, you're okay. It's just a scratch, you're not even bleeding. You're fine. Go back and play." And before you know it she's calmed down, feeling seen, understood, and reassured. The fear dissipates, and she runs off to play with her friends, leaving her worries behind.

Now, imagine the same scenario but dad is less calm when he meets her. "Oh NO!" he yells, "what happened!? Are you okay? Where are you bleeding? How badly does it hurt!?" As you might expect, his anxious reaction fuels her fears. She looks at him and thinks, "If an adult thinks it's a big deal, then it must be way worse than I thought. I'm definitely going to need a doctor. Maybe I'll have to get a NEEDLE!" Her fear has now grown tenfold, all because her place of safety, which is meant to be her dad, has responded with alarm. This version of dad has turned a "nothing" event into a full-blown crisis. As Shakespeare wrote in *Hamlet*, "There is nothing either good or bad, but thinking makes it so."

This example mirrors how your wife looks to you in moments of emotional stress. Just like that little girl, she wants to know if things are as bad as they seem. She really wants to hear—once she feels that she herself has been heard—that it's okay. That she's safe. The Storm wasn't her looking for a fight, it was her way of looking for reassurance that everything is manageable, and that she can go back to feeling at ease. It's your job to provide that.

You might reasonably ask why your wife has to Storm at you just to feel your strength. If she wants reassurance, why not just ask for it? But what you're essentially asking is why can't she be more like you. To see the world as you, a man, see it. In short, not to be herself. For her to change for you. But as we've already made clear, the only person you're able to change is yourself. Besides, most of the time your wife is not trying to manipulate you or make things hard. She genuinely feels overwhelmed. The Storm is *not* a conscious tactic. This is particularly important to remember when the Storm begins over something that seems trivial to you. It could be an empty beer bottle you've left on the counter or a McDonald's wrapper that's been in the car for a week. For you, a wrapper is just a wrapper. For your wife, when she's about to Storm, the wrapper (or whatever it is) symbolizes something bigger, like a lack of care or even a lack of love. When she feels unloved, her world begins to unravel, and she very well might Storm in your direction—and if you react defensively or get destabilized, she sees it as a confirmation of her fears. She thinks, "I knew it. I can tell by his reaction he doesn't care about me." In that moment she needed to feel the depth of your strength and your love, she needed calm reassurance during the Storm, but all she got was bigger waves. Now, this may seem ridiculous to the male brain, but I can promise you that enough of these interactions, stacked-up on each other for years, can end a marriage.

When she's throwing her emotions at you, she's testing whether you can remain steady. If you respond with grounded love and curiosity, seeking to understand how she's feeling and where she's coming from, she will calm down. She will think, "It's not as bad as I thought. It's okay. I can relax." On the other hand, if there's a real Storm in life—a crisis of some kind—she might want to know if she's with a man who can weather it. At a subconscious level she might even allow an emotional Storm to occur just to see if you can stand firm. And if you get rattled, she'll think, "If he can't stay calm now, with little old me complaining about a wrapper, what will happen when there's an actual crisis? *This man* cannot protect me, he's as unstable as I am!" Her level of perceived safety will drop, and things will get worse for both of you.

In both scenarios, what she's seeking is the safety of the masculine presence. She wants to know that she's with a man who can handle the things she can't, so she can relax, soften, and be nurturing. If she feels she has to be her own protection, she can't let down her guard, and she will lean on *her own internal masculine.*

She'll become more critical, more confrontational, and less able to be her true, nurturing self. But if she knows you're there—solid, grounded, unshakeable—then she can let herself be vulnerable, be feminine. This is what being a Lighthouse means: standing firm, being a calm, upright presence with a guiding light, especially in the middle of an emotional Storm, when it matters the most.

Don't get caught up in the details of her arguments. We'll dive deeper into this in later chapters, but for now, remember: ignore the specifics, ignore the bait. You can validate her underlying emotional reality without having to agree with what she says. Just because she says something is the end of the world doesn't make it so. What she needs from you is calm, and for you to be stronger than the Storm. Show her that strength, and she will find her own calm in your presence.

Storm Warning

If you find yourself being defensive, reactive, or unstable during an argument, it's a clear sign you're not being the Lighthouse. Check whether you're slouching, pouting, or lashing out in anger? Do you feel beaten down, afraid, or overwhelmed by her emotions? These are all warning signs that you're not standing steady. If you catch yourself taking shots at her, defensively trying to prove a point, or acting from a place of hurt rather than calm, then you've entered into your own feminine emotional Storm. Your own, internal feminine is now on the outside, you're wearing it for her to see. You are no longer a source of masculine safety and guidance. As you know, the Lighthouse doesn't sway; it doesn't get swept away by the tides of emotion. If you're feeling destabilized, that's an indication that you need to step back, regroup, and find your ground again.

Another sign you're not being the Lighthouse is if you feel a sense of dread or fear about the emotional confrontation. If you're afraid of her Storm or are trying to avoid it altogether, it means you're not standing firm. It means you are *hiding*. Avoidance can make you feel like you're preserving peace, but ultimately you are simply hiding from your own fears—and she knows this. She doesn't want you to run from the Storm; she *needs* you to be there—calm, patient, and unyielding. When you're reactive, defensive, or shrinking away, you're not offering the safe harbor she's looking for. You're feeding the Storm.

When you notice you're not being the Lighthouse, the first thing to do is take a few deep breaths. Slow, deliberate breaths can help calm your body and mind. There are hundreds of effective techniques, but the basic idea is to breathe with your belly, not your chest, and to make your exhales longer than your inhales. This type of breathing signals to your body that you are safe and activates your parasympathetic nervous system, helping you regain your calm. On top of this, physically ground yourself by planting your feet firmly on the floor. Stand taller, lift your chest, and raise your chin slightly. Roll back your shoulders. These physical adjustments signal to your nervous system that you are not in danger because you are not trying to hide your vital organs, in fact, you are confidently displaying their location. When you intentionally adopt a posture of strength, it helps shift your mindset as a result. Remind yourself of your role: you are here to be a source of calm, not to win an argument. By focusing on your breath and your posture, you can begin to settle your emotions and step back into your role as the Lighthouse.

Personal Experience

I've been through Storms with my wife, Whitney, many times. She'll come at me with something intense—a serious emotional Storm. She's not exactly a wallflower, so when she Storms… let's just say you can feel it. My natural tendency in those moments is to fire back: "You're wrong. You're not being fair. You're not giving me credit. You're not being appreciative or respectful." But I've learned that in those moments, this does not help.

She's not looking to be *right*. In my own mind, I often think that's what she's doing. My instinctive response is that she must be trying to prove a point. But then I remember that our minds work very differently. She's not interested in being factually correct, she's interested in finding a safe place to land.

So my role is to be a Lighthouse. My role is to show her that I am emotionally unflappable. Her Storm is not going to take me over or cause me to Storm back. It's not going to tip me over or destabilize me. I am rock solid. When I do this successfully—which, even after years of practice, is definitely not every time, because our wives can push our buttons like no one else—she eventually reaches a point where she... tires herself out. She gets all that turmoil out, releases all that pent up emotion. Sometimes that might take a few hours or it might even continue into the next day. As a man, sometimes you have to be *really* patient.

But once she gets there, she *always* comes back to me and says something like, "You are such an amazing husband, you were so good with me. I love you so much." She'll begin to explain why it wasn't actually as bad as it seemed, why some of what she said wasn't true, and apologize if she crossed any lines. By the end, she's calm, she's affectionate—she's grateful.

Most often, she shows her gratitude indirectly: affection, kind words, softness, or 'Bambi eyes.' She'll communicate her gratitude in whatever way women do—sometimes more obviously, sometimes subtly. And yes, very often in the way you might be thinking right now.... But the point is, she lets me know, verbally or nonverbally, "Hey, you stood strong for me, and that's what I needed. I'm grateful I have that support in you. *I feel better.*"

And, as a note of encouragement, when you get good at this, and when she trusts your stability, you can usually get from the Storm to the bedroom in 10-15 minutes, tops.

Take The Pressure, Not The Punches

Now, being the Lighthouse does not mean you're meant to be a punching bag. In the beginning, if there's a lot of pent-up resentment in the relationship—if you've done things that are hurtful and wrong and never owned up to them—then opening up and taking responsibility may initially make you feel like one.

In fact, she may need to release some of that resentment, and the faster she can let it out, the better it will be for both of you. However, in the long term, being the Lighthouse doesn't mean being passive. It's not about agreeing to all of her complaints and criticisms. Nor is it giving her a blank cheque so that she can do whatever she wants. Behaviors like gaslighting, manipulation, and false accusations are not acceptable and it's okay and very much necessary to maintain healthy boundaries. Very importantly—it's *being the Lighthouse* that puts you in a position to put your foot down, have reasonable expectations, and create healthy boundaries. This is something we'll talk more about in another chapter. But, for now, you must find a way to validate what she is *feeling* as she Storms, even if you don't agree with what she's *saying*. I know that's not easy, but nobody ever said marriages were easy—only that they're worth it.

The thing to keep hold of here is that while the Lighthouse can and should stand up for itself, it does so from a place of calm strength and masculine confidence. It absolutely is not about giving your wife permission to treat you poorly or being weak or passive. Rather, it's about being strong—so strong that you are bigger than the Storm, without needing to attack or be defensive. If you respond in kind, that just means you are *threatened* by the Storm, and all you do is throw yourself into it. The key, therefore, is to focus on validating how she feels and addressing her emotional needs with empathy, without necessarily agreeing to her factual analysis or personal demands. It's possible that she's correct, but you'll probably need to enter into calm reflection to figure that out. But she may also be wrong. She may only be saying these things to make her underlying emotional reality more vivid for you—not because she fully believes them herself. That's why you need to be, always, bigger than the Storm.

Curiosity And The Storm

Part of shining your light as a Lighthouse is simply listening to what she's saying. It's about asking her questions and showing genuine curiosity. Being curious is crucial when you're being a Lighthouse because what she really needs is to feel understood. It doesn't matter whether she's being factually accurate or not, contradictory or not (more on this later)—and she likely will be, because emotions can be messy and complex—the goal is to help her understand herself, not to understand you just yet. The fact that she's Storming to begin with is evidence that she may not fully understand what she's feeling. This is one of the reasons why it's helpful to ask gently clarifying questions. It helps her to get to the heart of the matter—and to better understand her own heart in the process.

This may take some time.

For men, finding the truth often feels like a straight line from A to B. But for women, it's more like a labyrinth. She needs time to find the center, and she might circle around the truth for a while before getting there. If you can stay calm and help guide her towards that center, towards the truth at the heart of what's bothering her, she will feel seen and understood. You'll give her the masculine gift of *clarity*. She'll think, "Wow, my man gets why this is such a big deal to me. He understands why leaving a wrapper on the passenger seat of my car feels like a big deal. He gets why that matters to me." And once she feels that you understand her, she might realize that maybe the wrapper isn't such a big deal after all. As you will see, when you meet her Storm with your Lighthouse, her original complaint almost always evaporates into thin air—because it was never about that to begin with. By the end she'll likely think, instead, "He's so wonderful, so desirable and strong—I'm so lucky to have him." In fact, she probably won't even remember why she was upset in the first place.

But if you try to convince her logically that the wrapper isn't a big deal, she's just going to think, "He doesn't get it, he doesn't understand me, he doesn't care about my feelings." And she'll escalate her emotions, trying to get you to understand just how important it feels. Her complaint will become *more real* to her, and *bigger*. So, be calm, be patient, and be grounded. Don't be passive—the Lighthouse is not a punching bag. But you don't need to get into a huge blow-up fight or argue about the details. Instead, meet her where she's at. Be loving, be curious, and let her know you're here for her, ugly emotions or not. Show her that you can rise above the situation and provide a place of safety. That *you are not threatened.* When she feels that safety, she can relax into her feminine energy, becoming nurturing and soft once more. This can likewise lead to more connection, more affection, and more intimacy. In short, more of the good stuff that we all want.

Takeaways

In every marriage, there will be Storms. The key is to be stronger than her chaos. Your role is not to fix the Storm or get caught in it but to provide the strength and stability your partner needs to feel safe. When you stand as the Lighthouse, you give her the reassurance that the Storm will pass, and everything will be okay. Remember, she's not attacking you. She's testing your strength. Because if you fall apart when she does… she can't trust you. And if she can't trust you, she can't relax into love. What she really needs is you. The steady, masculine, safe harbor in the middle of her emotional storm.

A Man's Work

Reading won't make you strong—rehearsal will. These two exercises train you to stand firm when storms hit your marriage. Don't wait for the next blow-up. Prepare now. Reflect, write, practise. The Lighthouse isn't born in calm seas—it's built through repetition. Do the work. Your future peace depends on it.

1) Storm Response Reflection (Journaling Prompt)

Instructions: You're her Lighthouse, not her Storm-chaser. Take 10 minutes to recall the last time she lost it—big or small. What happened? How did you react? What wound in you got triggered? Be honest. Then write in your notebook one way you could've stayed calm, steady, and loving. This is how you train.

Purpose: This builds awareness of reactive patterns and prepares you to stay grounded in conflict.

2) Storm Simulation

Instructions: Rehearse your role. Picture your wife in a Storm—snapping over something small. Visualize it clearly. Then write a 1-page script of you staying calm, validating her, and avoiding arguments. Practice aloud 2–3 times this week. This isn't pretend—it's how you build unshakable strength.

Purpose: This prepares you to handle emotional Storms with calm confidence, helping you to reinforce your role as The Lighthouse. Rather than being surprised and caught off-guard, you are prepared and practiced—your mind and body are in known territory.

Notes to Self

THE THIRD LAW:
DO NOT TAKE THE FACTBAIT

Core Differences

The last chapter introduced you to the theory of The Lighthouse and The Storm. This chapter is all about understanding her more deeply than she understands herself. It's about strategy. It's about you connecting with your partner, making her feel safe and understood—so that your differences don't escalate into disagreements and full-scale fights. This is crucial, because how you manage these differences will define your marriage. Master this and you'll be well on your way to becoming The Lighthouse. Don't, and you won't.

George Bernard Shaw once quipped that England and America are two countries divided by a common tongue. They both speak the same language, but they see the language differently. Husbands and wives are much the same, only more so. They inhabit the same world, but they see it differently. They *experience* it differently. This difference, more than anything else, can lead to divisions in a relationship. You've probably guessed what that difference is already, and I'm sure you've experienced the division I'm talking about—the heated arguments and ugly shouting matches. The difference is that husbands see situations through facts and wives see through their feelings. Neither is better, but both are very, very different.

Let's break this down a bit more. Men and women approach the world around them—and their relationships—differently. Men tend to navigate life by analyzing the facts of a situation. From there, they determine what belief makes the most sense and what action to take. For men, logic is the map, and decision-making is the destination. We then sublimate our feelings to this analysis. In other words, we analyze and *then* we feel. Women approach things from a different angle. They start by analyzing how they *feel* about a situation. Those feelings shape their beliefs, thoughts, and actions. Emotion isn't a detour; it's the starting point. They feel and then they analyze the facts *through that lens.*

For men to be happily married, they have to take this into account. They have to *work with it, not around it.* So, always remember this: in emotionally tense situations, a husband's facts won't change a wife's feelings—they'll only make her feelings even more intense, because she's desperately trying to make you see her underlying emotional reality… and you "don't care enough" to see it. You're concerned only with lifeless facts, not her heart, not her reality.

Let's be clear though, in case we have some dummies reading right now. This doesn't mean women are incapable of logical thinking. Of course not. If your wife is a scientist working in a lab, or a corporate manager analyzing a business decision, she's making decisions based on data, hypothesis testing, and logic just like anyone else. The key difference is what women do in the *context of a relationship.* When it comes to navigating conflict or addressing tension, men default to fact-mode and women double-down on their feelings. Understanding this difference is critical, because it informs everything—how you communicate, how you resolve conflict, and how you build trust and connection. Get this and you've got a firm foundation to build on.

It Goes Deep

I know this approach isn't easy. As men, we place huge importance on being both morally right and factually accurate. That's because we're taught from a young age—and thank God we are—to sublimate our feelings to our principles and beliefs. To channel our strong emotions and physical strength towards our principles. We're reminded that might doesn't make right and that the pen is mightier than the sword. We're taught this because on average men are more inclined to violence. We're more threatening than women. Even as three- or four-year-olds we're causing damage around the house and often hurting our siblings and sometimes even our parents. But through these experiences, we hopefully realize, *Oh man, I can really harm people. I have to be careful, because when I lose my self-control, very bad things can happen!* So that's why we build boundaries to help us avoid acting too impulsively—developing the principles we need to restrain ourselves and the rational thinking required to regulate us. And it's this ability to govern our emotions through our principles that prevents both personal and societal chaos. Without it, the world would quickly become a very violent and dangerous place. Men controlled by emotions—men possessed by their own feminine emotional storm—are unstable and often destructive.

Women, however, don't learn the same lesson in childhood. On average, they aren't as physically capable of violence as men. They don't grow up needing to suppress their emotions to avoid causing physical harm. For them, feelings take precedence over principles. That's why we say, women act from the heart while men act from the head. There's truth in that.

Because women prioritize feelings, the facts in a given situation become subordinate to how they feel. As such, a woman's view of her own relationship can change as quickly as her mood. If she feels disconnected, the tint of her emotions makes everything darker. In such a moment, you've "always" been disconnected. The sex has "never" been good. You've "never" been there for her. The future looks as bleak as the present—only infinitely worse. But if she begins to feel safe, seen and connected again—then her emotional outlook becomes rosier. The sex has always been amazing. You're the best at being there for her and as far as the future is concerned, you're soulmates and you always will be. My guess is you have experienced this and, while reading, recalled *more* than one encounter where you dealt with this phenomenon.

As Sting once sang, a woman can be all four seasons in one day. Obviously, this doesn't make life easy for men, but it's not something that's about to change. This is how women process the world.

In so many ways it's their gift to the world, as it fosters greater empathy, creativity, and human connectedness. It's also how they navigate their marriages—and unless you're a man married to another man, you're going to have to get *with this* rather than around it. So, the next time your wife unexpectedly overreacts about the dirty dishes, don't pull out your 'dishes log' and show her that you cleaned the kitchen 17 out of the last 20 times. In a situation like this, the dishes aren't the real issue. You're going to need to dodge those 'facts'. Forget about them for now—you can show her your dishwashing stats when her Love Switch (more on that later) has turned back on. But if you fight with her over the facts now, you'll only invalidate her feelings, which will only exacerbate her need to be seen, and the fight will escalate.

Her Reality Is Just As Real

For women, feelings are as central to their identity as beliefs are for men. Just as you might feel deeply hurt when your beliefs are dismissed or disrespected, women feel the same when their emotions are invalidated. When you dismiss her feelings—even if those feelings are tied to inaccurate facts—you're sending the message that you don't see her, don't love her, and don't care about who she is. So, instead of correcting her, you can say: "Hey, I want to know what you're feeling right now. What do you need from me? What do you need me to recognize? I know this must be really hard for you and I'm here for you." By doing this, you show her that you care about her reality. You're not there to win an argument or prove her wrong. You're simply there. For her.

Here's a little story to illustrate my point. Some time back, I was downstairs in our basement when I heard a clatter upstairs in the kitchen. This was followed by the voice of my daughter, Aria, shouting "Daddy, why did you make me spill the milk!?" Obviously, I had nothing to do with the milk being spilled, but for whatever reason it was my fault. Perhaps she thought I should have been there as some kind of milk-like life guard, but I don't know. Either way, she was upset. The important thing is that I didn't get emotional when she blamed me. I didn't feel threatened or outraged. I just went upstairs and gave her a huge bear hug. I said, "Daddy's here for you." In much the same way, a grown-up woman is just like that. Her metaphorical milk has been spilled and she's projecting the problem onto you. She's latching onto what she knows and whom she loves—which is you—hoping that you'll be there to reassure her. The milk itself is unimportant, but the reassurance she's looking for is important. When I did this for my daughter, she hugged me back and said without any prompting, "Daddy, I know you didn't spill the milk." The point here is that the facts didn't matter. Me being there, solid, present, loving, did.

When you approach your wife this way, everything changes. Instead of reacting defensively or getting stuck in the details, you're saying: *I get it. I see that you're overwhelmed right now. I understand that your friend's cousin is in the hospital with cancer, and that's weighing on you. I see that something at work upset you, and that's still on your mind. I see that this vacation planning has hit a snag, and now you're stressed about finding a new hotel. I understand you're juggling all these things, and it feels like too much.* By acknowledging her feelings, you show her that you're strong enough to wrap your arms around her and say "I'm here for you". You're not getting defensive, reactive, or trying to 'fix' her facts. Instead, you're saying, *It's okay. I'm here. I can handle this.* And that's what she needs most: your steady presence, your validation of her emotions, and your willingness to meet her where she is.

When you do that, you create the emotional safety she craves, and the connection between you will deepen. Now your differences won't escalate into a drawn-out argument—both of you insisting the other is wrong, letting the tension drag on for hours, days, weeks, or even months. Instead, you'll start resolving things more quickly. In the beginning, this process might take a little longer, maybe half an hour or an hour. But as you practice and get better at it, conflicts can be resolved in just a few minutes or even a single moment.

When you do this well, she will usually soften and fall into your arms. She may not explicitly say, "I'm sorry, I was wrong," but she'll express it in her own way. Maybe she'll be a little extra affectionate, give you a compliment, or treat you with the warmth and respect that shows she feels apologetic—even if she doesn't say the exact words. When that happens, you'll know: *This is what she needed.* She needed to feel that recognition. At that point, she'll often begin to talk herself out of her original complaints. She might say something like, "Well, it doesn't actually matter about this," or, "I know I said that, but it's not really a big deal." She'll naturally soften her stance on the things she initially brought up, because those issues were only extensions of her feelings in the moment.

The Immovable and The Unstoppable

To help illustrate what I mean, let's imagine the following scenario. Your wife gets home after a long day. You've been with the kids for a couple of hours, and as she walks through the door, you can tell she's stressed out of her mind. Her first words? "Why isn't the kitchen clean? The floor's not tidy. The dog hasn't been taken out. Why aren't the kids in their pajamas?"

Your immediate reaction is to try to stay calm and avoid conflict. You think, *Okay, I'm going to handle this properly.* So you respond with a logical explanation: "I haven't done the floors yet because I wanted to clean the table first and usually crumbs fall off the table, so it made sense to do that first. The dishes aren't done because I'm about to make the kids a snack, and I'll clean up everything afterward. The dog's already been taken out, so that's not an issue. And the kids aren't in their pajamas because it's only 6:45—I never put them in pajamas until 7:30 anyway, so there's plenty of time."

You think to yourself, *Boom, nailed it! I just deconstructed everything calmly, reasonably, and factually. I showed her there's no reason to be stressed.* But instead of her saying, "Oh wow, good point. Sorry, my bad—let's start over," she escalates. She gets more tense, more stressed, and even more upset. Her emotional intensity, inexplicably, rises. From your perspective, this makes no sense. You gave a rational explanation, and she responded irrationally. Naturally, you think, *It's her fault. She's the one being unreasonable, not me.* And from a solely male perspective, you're correct. This is the kind of thing that drives men absolutely crazy. I'll explain what is actually happening here shortly, but first we are going to talk about the importance of learning more about her language of communication.

Think about it this way. If your best friend only speaks Mandarin, and you want to be close, you're going to have to learn Mandarin. You could ignore their language and demand they learn yours—try to force them to meet you where you're comfortable—but that's not how real friendship works. If you did that, the relationship would suffer. Marriage is no different. If you want your marriage to work, you need to learn how she operates—meet her on her level. Over time, you can help her to understand how you operate and you can learn to both speak each other's language—but it starts with you. Not because it's your fault, in fact, there is a very good chance you are a much clearer communicator, but because men need to be the leaders in their own lives and in their relationships. So, here is what is actually happening when she responds to your reasonable explanation with a chaotic storm.

Emotional Realities

Just to make sure we've really got this, let's return to the scenario above.

Your wife walks through the door and starts hurling emotions at you. You stay calm, try to explain things logically, thinking surely that will clear it up. But it doesn't. Why? Because the emotional charge she's bringing into this moment didn't start at the door. It started long before she got home—hours ago, maybe days. Something was building. Something was festering. And now it's spilling over.

That means the facts of the situation—believe it or not—are largely irrelevant. She might be criticizing you about the dishes, but it's not really about the dishes. The dishes are just the tip of the iceberg. The trigger. What matters is what she *feels* the dishes represent: a lack of support, neglect, being unseen, being alone in her burdens. She's not reacting to the chore. She's reacting to what the chore *means* to her in that moment.

She's seeing the dishes and everything else in this situation through different lenses than you.

In this scenario, instead of throwing a list of logical explanations at her, try to meet her on an emotional level. At this moment she's likely feeling overwhelmed and unsupported, like everything is too much. So begin with acknowledging how she's really feeling. This might mean saying something like: "Hey, babe, I can sense you're feeling a bit overwhelmed right now. I just want you to know, I'm here for you. I've got this handled—you don't need to worry about any of it. I know you've got a lot on your plate right now... Why don't you just go to your room, get changed, and take a minute to relax? I'm on top of all of this."

Notice what's missing? You haven't addressed *any* of the factual concerns she raised. You haven't explained why the kids aren't in pajamas or the kitchen isn't clean (because you'd likely be wasting your breath). Instead, you've addressed her emotional reality—and that's what she truly needs in that moment. You're offering her solidarity, not a solution. Try this, and just *watch* what happens. Now, if we reverse the roles, when a husband complains he's usually looking for his wife to confirm his version of the facts. He wants to hear her say, "Yeah, I see what you're saying. That's a valid point." But it's not the same when the shoe's on the other foot. When she's stressed and venting, she's not looking for a factual analysis. Deep down, she's looking for *recognition of how she's feeling*. You need to provide that. Because once she feels like you 'get it', that you 'get her', that *you're connected*, that's when she'll trust that you've got the other stuff handled too. *The facts of the original complaint will likely evaporate* like water on hot asphalt. But this won't happen if you respond to her feelings with your facts, because addressing her issues isn't the same as addressing her underlying emotions. In order to feel *reassured by you*, she needs to feel *connected with you*.

Dodge The Facts, Address The Feelings

What tends to happen is that when you engage with her on an emotional level—acknowledging what she's feeling—the long list of 'facts' she presented dissolves. Those specific issues she mentioned may suddenly seem far less pressing to her. She might even say something like, "You know what? The dishes don't matter, the dog isn't a big deal, and the kids are fine for now..." Why? Because deep down, she probably knew those things already, and she's viewing the situation through emotional lenses—only now things are much rosier because she's feeling reassured and connected. But this wouldn't have happened if you'd prioritized the facts over her feelings. In reality, if you engage with her complaints on a factual level, it just means her feelings remain unaddressed. As a result, she will begin to generate an even longer list of facts and complaints in a desperate attempt to get you to see what she's feeling. This is why, and I know you've experienced this, when you logically address the facts of her complaints, she immediately generates ten new complaints. Addressing the facts is like cutting the heads off the mythical Hydra—for every fact you address, two more grow in its place.

So, if she throws her own version of the facts at you—complaints, observations, or to-dos—your first job is to set those aside. Dodge them like Neo dodging bullets in the Matrix. Don't disprove them. Don't deconstruct them. Just side-step them for the time being. She's coming from a place of feelings, and that is where you need to meet her. If you don't, it will reinforce her internal sense that you don't understand her. She's thinking, *He doesn't see what I'm feeling. He doesn't grasp how much this matters to me, how overwhelmed I am, or how much pain I'm in. He can't even see me.* Nothing good will come from this because when she feels unseen her emotional state escalates. The tension rises. The conflict intensifies.

But if you can resist the fact-bait she's thrown at you and instead engage with her on the level of her feelings, you'll notice a *powerful and positive shift in her emotional state.* This is when her Love Switch begins to turn back on, which is something we'll discuss more in another chapter. When this happens—and this is important to know—she's capable of thinking logically again. You can think about it this way: when her emotional brain is overactive, her logical brain turns off. So you have to help her emotional brain settle before you can tackle things together from a logical perspective. When you do that, it's now safe for you to talk about some of those erroneous or unfair facts she threw your way—though you might not even need to do so because, as you'll see, she didn't really care about them that much to begin with. When you truly understand this, you'll think to yourself, *It doesn't really matter. I know she didn't mean it literally when she said I never do the dishes.* And the next day, she'll probably thank you for being so great at helping with the dishes—because now she feels connected again, and the facts that stand out to her are different as a result.

So, here's the bottom line: *Dodge the facts, address the feelings.* That's the root of her concerns and the place where she lives. Don't get into a debate over the details. That's not where resolution happens and you'll frustrate the crap out of yourself. You don't win by proving you're correct, you win by meeting her on the level of her feelings. That's how you create connection, defuse conflict, and build a stronger relationship. This is how you bridge the divide that exists between you—that, to some degree, will always exist between you. Do this and you will experience not only *way less frustration* but also *way more connection.*

A Man's Work

This chapter has been about shifting from defense to presence. These three exercises train your mind and body to lead with calm, not control. You'll learn to hear her heart, not just her words. As always, the key here is not just to read the chapter. That's the easy part. Now do the work, because kings practice what they preach.

1) Fact vs. Feeling

Instructions: Recall a recent argument where you clung to facts. What did you say? How did she react? Now, ask: What was she feeling underneath? In your notebook, write one validating sentence you could've said. Do this after future arguments to train your empathy and dodge defensive reflexes.

Purpose: This enhances your awareness of fact-based reactivity and builds empathy for emotional needs.

2) Role Reversal Reflection

Instructions: Step into her shoes. Pick a conflict and write a one-page version from her perspective. Focus on how she felt (not what she said). No edits—just honesty. Then, write one action you'll take next time to meet that emotional need (e.g., "I'll ask how she's feeling before explaining.") Practice this weekly to rewire how you listen and respond.

Purpose: This develops empathy for your wife's emotional lens, helping you to see beyond facts to her feelings.

3) Breathwork (Wim Hof Method)

Instructions: Your breath fuels strength. Sit or lay down. Take

30 deep breaths with relaxed exhales, then exhale and hold empty lungs for as long as possible. Inhale, hold 15 seconds, repeat 2–3 rounds. Do this daily or before tough talks. You're not just calming down—you're training to hold your ground with power and peace.

Purpose: This enhances resilience and focus for enforcing boundaries and will reset your nervous system through practice.

Notes to Self

THE FOURTH LAW: FLIP THE LOVE SWITCH

+

THE FIFTH LAW: LIGHTEN HER MOOD GLASSES

What You See Is What You Get

Human vision is an extraordinary thing. The eyes see by capturing light that reflects off objects. That reflected light enters through the cornea and pupil, which gets focused by the lens onto the retina at the back of the eye. The retina's rods and cones convert light into electrical signals, which travel through the optic nerve to the brain—enabling us to see everything from the redness of an apple to the shape of Homer Simpson's beer belly. We forget how amazing this is, because it happens all the time. But in actual fact, it doesn't happen for everyone, not all the time. Not only do some people suffer from color blindness—mistaking red for green or yellow for violet—but there are some people who have it even worse. There are some who can't see any color at all. This is called achromatopsia. Those who have it can only see the world as black and white or in many different shades of grey—though probably not fifty shades… This is a rare phenomenon, and it's usually permanent, but for some people their vision can alternate between both color and black and white.

I'd like you to imagine for a moment what it would be like to have your entire view of reality shift from one moment to the next. As a man, it might be difficult to fully appreciate how strange that would be. For a woman, however, it might not be as difficult as you'd expect. That's not because more women are colorblind (quite the opposite, in fact), rather, it's because women often experience more fundamental shifts in their outlook than men do. One reason for this is that women—especially in the context of relationships—relate to things based on their (often changing) emotions. For instance, in a marriage, if a wife feels happy, healthy, and emotionally connected to her husband, things are good. Indeed, things have never been so great. Better yet, things have always been this amazing! But if she's not happy, healthy, and feeling connected, then not only are things terrible, they've always been terrible. And then, after all that—much to her husband's happy yet confused amazement—she can change back just as quickly, and all is well with you and the world again. At this point, you'd be forgiven for wondering *what the hell is happening?*

The answer is a two-parter, but it's straightforward enough. It's because her Love Switch is flicking on and off, and it's because she's viewing the world through her Mood Glasses. Taken together, these two concepts will help to explain why your wife often relates to you and to the world around her in ways that don't make sense to you. How it is that she can be warm and loving one moment, then distant and uncaring the next. How everything in her life can be wonderfully rosy in the morning, but then absolutely rubbish by the afternoon. In short, how she can seem to fall in and out of love with you so quickly—and not just you, but potentially anything, and sometimes everything.

The Love Switch

I learned about the concept of the Love Switch in Alison Armstrong's amazing seminar, *Understanding Women: Unravelling the Mystery*. It's available as an audiobook, and if you're serious about understanding your wife in the context of your relationship, I *highly* recommend you listen to it. It's worth every penny. Indeed, not only is Alison an absolutely wonderful person, but it was her who first opened my eyes to just how differently men and women experience love. A lot of what follows is inspired by her work, though I've added substantial nuances of my own.

For men, the Love Switch is straightforward. It flicks on during the dating phase or around the time of engagement. Once it's on, it stays on. You love your new wife and that's that. In time, she may do things that drive you mad or make you angry—but your love for her is bedrock. It would take a lot, like betrayal or prolonged, repeated negativity from her for your Love Switch to turn off. Even then, if an intruder came through the door of your home, you'd probably defend your wife, because the love you feel for her is pretty constant—even if that love is sometimes felt alongside other, more negative emotions. But yes, a man's Love Switch *can* turn off but typically only after intense amounts of pain in a relationship. And when that happens for men, the switch is unlikely to flip back on.

For women, it's completely different. A woman's Love Switch can flip on and off—many times. And not just over the course of her marriage, but even in a single day. This can be confusing—often painful—for men, who are used to their more stable, all-or-nothing Love Switch. It's not uncommon for a man to think, "Wait, weren't we in love just yesterday? What changed?" That's an entirely reasonable question and one that we're going to address, but for your marriage to work, you're going to need to come to terms with the way your wife's Love Switch works. The good news is that these off-switch moments are temporary and often unrelated to her deeper, enduring love for you. It's a question of how she feels, not what she thinks. But don't try to be an electrician, because her switch isn't broken—it's just different than yours. It's not worse. It's not better. It's just different. And remember, it's how we work with these differences, rather than trying to work against or around them, that makes the difference in a marriage. Accepting the rules of the game and playing your best within them is a much more effective life strategy than railing against reality for being… well, reality.

Let's dig into this a bit deeper. Even in a healthy relationship, your wife's Love Switch might flick off two, three, or even five times in a single day. When she's feeling super connected to you, she feels deeply in love. Head over heels. On cloud nine. You're the best man she's ever been with. You're the only man for her. Then she might come across a pair of dirty pants that you've thoughtlessly left on the floor and suddenly she feels less connected. Less appreciated. More exasperated. The Love Switch turns off. This doesn't mean that she no longer loves you, but it does mean that in that moment she doesn't actively feel love towards you. The deep, abiding love that comes from years' worth of marriage is still there, but it's not being felt. Like an actual light switch, when it's off it doesn't mean the wiring and electricity are damaged or in danger, they're just not being utilized. They're not being *felt*. It's the same for your wife.

The good(ish) news is that you're not alone in this. Not only is this true for all husbands, even if they're happily married. It's true for women as well, because this happens in their friendship groups. Whether it's the playground or the boardroom, female friendship groups are warm and loving—so long as a woman's in good standing. But look out if she falls out with them. Suddenly, the group closes ranks. One moment Suzie's part of the dream team, the next she's a public enemy. Her secrets get spilled. She gets nothing but bad press. But then—plot twist—something else happens and Suzie is back-in. Now, it's like she never left. Everyone loves Suzie. The girls have nothing but good things to say about her. In fact, *it's almost as if it never happened.* This is a constant mystery to men, but it isn't actually mysterious at all. It's just the Love Switch flicking off and on—only this time, it's not directed at you.

Complications

The Love Switch is a simple concept, but that doesn't mean it's always straightforward. A man can do one thing one day, and as far as his wife is concerned, he's in the clear. But he could do the same thing another day and his wife might react totally differently. For example, your wife cooks you dinner but she accidentally overcooks the meat. You mention in passing that the meat was overdone. Fortunately for you, her Love Switch is turned on: she takes it in her stride and if anything, she feels extra motivation to make the best damned dinner next time—because she loves you and thinks you deserve great meals. But when her Love Switch is off and you make the same remark, things don't go so well.

One possible scenario is that she interprets your remark as a subtle (or not so subtle!) indication that you don't love her anymore. She thinks that your switch has turned off. She now fears that you won't be there for her—to comfort her, provide for her, and defend her. But in another scenario, instead of just being hurt she becomes angry. She thinks you're incredibly ungrateful. That you don't appreciate the hard work she puts in on your behalf. Worse, not only are you an ungrateful husband, you're undeserving too. Who are you to demand perfection when you're such an imperfect spouse? Now she doesn't want to cook for you *ever again*—and good luck getting her to do anything else for you *ever again* either.

Regardless of the scenario—and these are just two possibilities—you're probably thinking *all that from a comment about the meat!? My God!* But, remember, it's not about the meat! The facts don't apply here. It's about the Love Switch. Just as a room can be plunged into darkness by the flip of a switch, so her view of your marriage can quickly turn from light to dark if her Love Switch flicks off.

That's one complication, which obviously isn't enough, so here's another. When your wife's Love Switch is turned off, she won't just feel things that surprise you, she may say things that shock you. Continuing with the overcooked meat, she might give you a piece of her mind. She might tell you straight up that you're no good. That you're too demanding. That you're unappreciative. If things get really heated, she might even say she needs a break from you. That "this"—you guys, your marriage—isn't working. Naturally, you'd be devastated if you heard this. Confused, too. But here she is—saying it—and you take it to heart. You believe her, interpreting her through your masculine lens, and as a result, you believe the relationship is doomed.

But here's the thing—and this is very, very important. In a

situation like this, she's not understanding you in the same way that you understand yourself—hence some of the confusion—but even more importantly, you're misunderstanding her. You're reacting as if she's you. That her Love Switch works the same as yours. That if it turns off, it turns off forever. But that's not how a woman's Love Switch works. In all reality, it could turn back on just as easily—especially if you take the lessons from this book on board. So here's the thing, when you recognize that your wife's Love Switch has turned off, *you must NOT take what she says at face value.* Instead, like The Lighthouse in The Storm, you need to keep shining your light, especially in the darkness. Remember, that *is* what lights are for.

We've All Been There

Every man who's been in a challenging relationship has likely heard something extreme from his wife during an 'off moment'. She might say the relationship is not working. That it's never worked. Or that she's not happy. That she's never been happy. Perhaps that your sex life isn't good and it's never been good (which is a common one I hear from the men that I work with). That _____ is _____… I trust that you can fill in the gaps yourself, because you've surely experienced something like this. No doubt you've also taken it to heart. That you've been wounded and feared the worst. That you've wondered how the relationship could ever get back on track, because when men hear these things, they filter them through their own masculine matrix. What men hear are factual pronouncements—final, irrevocable truths about reality itself. We think, "Oh no, it's over. Why else would she say something so extreme unless she deeply meant it?"

But here's the reality: she doesn't deeply mean it. She deeply *feels* it—in that moment. But there's a crucial distinction. When her Love Switch is off, her emotions alter her reality. This doesn't mean it's a false reality, just that it's only a temporary one. Just how temporary depends on the situation, but you'd be amazed at what a little love or a little goofiness can do. This may sound cheesy, but try picking her up and spinning her around. Give her a bear hug. Do whatever: tickle her, crack a joke, or get her flowers. The point is that whichever action you choose, doing it with the right intention—something fun, caring and/or connecting—will help turn the switch back on. When that happens, all of her extreme thoughts and words will vanish like smoke (and likely won't require a three-hour conversation to resolve).

When her Love Switch is off, resist the urge to panic or take her words as permanent truths. This isn't the time to bring up a big issue in your relationship, or to get out of Dodge by asking for a weekend away with the boys. Avoid the urge to resolve deep-seated conflicts (this one is important!). Instead, focus on grounding her. Be present. Affirm her. Help her get back into her body—whether that is because she's now laughing or singing, being hugged or held in the air—as this will help create a positive emotional space. Once she's feeling things like joy, security, and warmth the Love Switch will flip back on, because she's back to feeling connected and in love with you.

Warning Signs

Once you recognize the Love Switch dynamic, so much of her behavior starts to make sense. Nevertheless, the constant flicking on and off can take you by surprise until you've learned to clearly identify the signs. This was definitely true at an earlier stage in my own marriage. I'd be out on a date and everything would be going great. My wife would be raving about the restaurant, loving her entrée, marveling at the dessert menu, and genuinely excited about what's to come. Dessert arrives, and she enjoys it. All is well. Then, five minutes later, something shifts. Suddenly, she seems distant, cold, like she's a million miles away. She starts saying the dinner wasn't that good, that now probably isn't the best time to be going on dates, that perhaps this was a bad idea, that I picked the wrong restaurant. On the drive home, she's quiet, staring out the window, barely speaking. Naturally, I would be thinking "What the hell just happened?" But then, by the time we're home, it's as if a completely different person has emerged. Suddenly, she's telling me it was a wonderful date, that she had so much fun, she loves me, and she's ready to hop into bed. And I'm left wondering, "Hold on, what just happened here? What was that?"

Fortunately, I'm better positioned now to see what was at work. That was just my wife's Love Switch at work. It flicked off for a while—probably because I ordered the bill while she was still eating, which for her came across as *proof* that I was having a terrible time—but then it flicked back on later. Likewise, I don't need to worry that it's some quirk associated only with my wife, because it's a near-universal experience for women. Before, I would have taken her comments (i.e. 'the facts') seriously. I'd be hurt: disappointed that the date wasn't a success, and then confused when it was again. Like any man, I would have tried to fix the problem. To come up with solutions. Now, I know better. Now, I know to weather the Storm and to shine my guiding light.

The same goes for you. When your wife's Love Switch is off, your job isn't to solve everything. It's to help her flick the switch back on. Maybe that means offering some lightheartedness, a bit of affection, or just giving her space to process her feelings. There's no one-size-fits-all here. But whatever you do, don't overanalyze or internalize the criticisms she might voice in those off-switch moments. They're not reflective of the deeper truths of your relationship—they're a product of the moment.

That said, it's a different story if she's expressing serious concerns when her Love Switch is on. If she's saying the relationship isn't working, or she's considering divorce while her Love Switch is on, that's when you need to pay close attention and take action. Those statements signal deeper issues that must be addressed. If you're in doubt, trust whatever she tells you (for good or bad) when the Love Switch is on—when she's engaged and warm—rather than putting too much stock into whatever she tells you when it's definitely off—when she's acting cold, distant, or resentful from out of the blue. It will take some practice, but in time you'll become like the weatherman: easily distinguishing between the weather, which can change day to day, and the climate, which only changes with the seasons.

For now, start with listening to both what your wife says and *how she says it*. This isn't an ironclad rule, but if your wife sits you down for a serious conversation about the problems in your marriage, it is much more significant than if she said something unexpectedly, out of context, and off the cuff. If it's the former, take heed. Be serious and take her seriously. If it's the latter, don't jump to immediate conclusions. Remember, this is the Love Switch at work. So don't worry, because *she's not about to file for divorce*. You might have a bumpy flight ahead, but the emotional turbulence is only temporary. Indeed, like an actual plane, if you can steer your wife's emotions to a higher altitude—back to feeling happy, secure, and connected—you should be able to avoid the turbulence entirely.

Doing this is vitally important. If the Love Switch is off more often than it's on, or if it stays off for longer and longer stretches, then your relationship will definitely deteriorate. If she spends too much time with her Love Switch turned off, she'll eventually reach a breaking point. At that point, she may feel like the only way to reclaim her happiness is to leave the marriage entirely. This doesn't necessarily mean it's over. In our coaching program we've saved countless marriages that were on the brink of divorce—including many, many couples who were already separated and living apart (even continents apart). But this underscores how important it is for you, as her husband, to learn how to turn her Love Switch back on.

Mood Glasses

To do this, you'll need to know about more than just the Love Switch. You need to know about her Mood Glasses. These are the lenses through which she sees the world. The tint of these lenses is dictated entirely by her emotions. If she feels rosy, the world is rosy too. If her mood is dark, everything is shrouded in darkness too. Now, you might be thinking that's not so different from you. When your mood is good, everything looks good and vice versa. But here's the thing. A woman's Mood Glasses impact how she sees the past, the present, and the future. In the context of your marriage, if she is feeling connected to you in that moment, then not only is the relationship healthy, *it's always been healthy and it will only become even healthier over time.*

For a husband, this is a great position to be in. Nobody is perfect, but as far as she's concerned, your past mistakes are forgotten, your present shortcomings are forgiven, and as far as the future is concerned, things look fine. In fact, better than fine. They look positively great! But let's switch things up. Her mood has suddenly shifted because she's feeling disconnected from you. This dims the tint of her Mood Glasses. Now, everything has a darkened hue. Now, everything looks bleak—including yesterday, today, and tomorrow. In this moment, she genuinely feels that you've never truly clicked, never had the deep bond she's always longed for. She might even compare your relationship (or, perhaps more painfully, your sex) unfavorably to her past boyfriends or her friends' marriages. And if the past was bad and the present is worse, then the future looks... hopeless. Even pointless.

This is very important to remember when she makes statements about how she *knows* it could never work between the two of you. How she has *always known* you weren't sexually compatible and you've *only* ever had bad sex. How you have *never* supported her financially, with the kids, in her career, etc. You have to remind yourself in these moments that she doesn't actually mean it. If you don't, you'll get bogged down in fruitless cross-examination: trying to reconcile (or contradict) her negative remarks with positive ones she's made in the past. But this won't get you far, because you're literally trying to reconcile opposites—which is a recipe (especially with men) for instant frustration and intense outbursts of anger.

Where before she felt you could do no wrong, now she feels like you can do nothing right. If she's feeling unsupported, then her Mood Glasses make her believe you've never supported her. You've never done the dishes, never helped with the kids, and never taken her needs seriously. Of course, you know that's not true. But here's the key: when she's wearing those glasses, facts don't matter. You could remind her of every loving gesture, every date, every moment she's told you how much she loves and appreciates you—but it won't make a dent. She simply can't see it. She can't *feel it*. But as you should know by now, the solution isn't to argue with her feelings. Don't waste your breath trying to "prove" how connected or supportive you are. Instead, focus on helping her feel connected. Help her change her Mood Glasses.

You Have The Power

The rate at which a woman's Love Switch and Mood Glasses can change bewilders many a man. If this describes you, know that you're not alone. I get complaints like this in my coaching program *every single day*. It's not unusual to hear on a Monday that a man's wife wants to divorce him and then by Tuesday that she's talking about them buying a house together or having another child. As you'd expect, these guys experience a lot of emotional whiplash—but the one thing they shouldn't feel is helpless. These men are not alone and nor are you. In fact, you have the power within you to change this entire dynamic.

As we've already discussed, your first task is to avoid the fact-bait. As before, this isn't a situation that needs you to come up with a new solution. It's not a problem that you can fix. Instead, it's time for taking action. But what you need to do isn't rocket science. You don't need a PhD in relationship counselling. Just go do something nice for her. It's as simple as that. Elevate her mood, be it with kindness, humor, or a fun activity. Doing this is completely within your power. Indeed, as you'll quickly discover when you see the results—it's your super power.

The next time her Love Switch is off and/or her darkened Mood Glasses are on, tell her to go to her room, have a glass of wine, and watch that crappy TV show she loves (and you hate). Furthermore, while she's doing that, take the kids to the park, or clean up the kitchen and give her a break from it all. Or, if eating out is more her thing, take her to her favorite restaurant—the one that's a little out of your budget but will go a long way. If it's reading, take her to the book store. If she loves hikes, go hiking together. Whatever it is, just do something that you know will help make her feel more alive again. More herself. Something that gets her out of her head and back into her senses. Something that reconnects you, because when she feels good again, her Love Switch will flick on and her Mood Glasses will become rosy.

When that happens, everything changes. Suddenly, the idea of divorce is totally crazy to her. The thought that you two could be disconnected in the future? Insane. How could that ever happen? Because right now—*in this moment*—she feels connected to you. And to her, that feeling *is reality*. It represents the past, the present, and the future. In that moment her feelings *are* the history of the relationship and *are* the future of the relationship.

Practice Makes Perfect

Back in the day, when Whitney and I hit a Storm, I used to jump right into it with her. Because I didn't stay out of the Storm, serving as The Lighthouse, her emotional Storms eventually lasted for days, and the disconnection could last weeks or months. At the time, I didn't know any better, but now I do. These days, even if she's in the middle of a particularly bad Storm—throwing "tests" at me (more on this later), saying things that make no sense, or just having "one of those days"—I stay calm. I don't get distracted by the facts. I don't take her words as gospel truth or assume she means them in some permanent sense. Instead, I skip past all of that. I joke with her. I playfully make fun of what she's saying, in a way that lets her pause, step back, and start to see the humor in it. Laughter might not work for your wife—every marriage is unique—but it works with mine. As a result, her feelings start to shift. She starts to laugh. Ten minutes later, everything's amazing again. She thinks I'm a great husband, and the emotional Storm is a distant memory.

And yes—once the Storm has passed, it often ends with really good sex. You'll notice that's a common theme with many of the concepts in this book. But that's not (only) why I do it—and nor should you—though let's be honest: it's a nice bonus. In a similar way, when you get really good at this you'll see the warning signs of an approaching Storm much sooner and with greater accuracy than before. You'll learn to recognize whether her Love Switch has changed and which Mood Glasses she has on. Then you'll know that now's not the time to engage her feelings with your facts. That you don't need to argue with her—but elevate her.

Get your wife back into her body, feeling positive and connected. In turn, that connection and safety will, over time, lead to much deeper sexual intimacy—magical, powerful intimacy that only comes from the polarity that you are providing. Indeed, the next time the Storm starts to pick up, you'll probably hear yourself thinking *she's acting a little crazy right now... and that probably means we're going to have amazing sex later.* Trust me, I've seen this countless times in every type of bad marriage you can imagine. This is *common*.

The bottom line is not about the sex, though. It's the fact that when her Love Switch is off and her darkened Mood Glasses are on, you don't have to take to heart the potentially hurtful things that she tells you. Don't waste time comparing yourself to her ex-lovers or worrying that you are a failure because you haven't bought her a nicer car. Don't take the passing eruptions too seriously. There's plenty of hard, honest work that you need to do as a husband—but believing the worst that your wife says about you in these moments isn't a part of it.

This means you're not obligated to accept her temporary emotional state as permanent reality. You're not in a courtroom, so you don't need to make a defence. There's no need for a cross-examination. You don't need to convince her to stay for the children's sake or spell out the financial ramifications of splitting up. Why? Number one, because it won't work. It'll likely just make her feel like she needs to escalate whatever she is saying to get you to see how she's feeling. And number two, because it's *unnecessary*. It's a waste of your time, it will likely make you frustrated, and there are far more *effective* ways of getting back to happiness for both of you. Like St Paul once said, you need to be the love, the joy, the peace, the patience, the kindness, the goodness, the faithfulness, the gentleness and the self-control.

Your focus needs to be on shifting her emotional state—to help her put on new glasses and flip that switch back on. Not just for her sake, but for yours too. *You don't need to waste your time arguing with the wind.* And when you get good at this, you'll be amazed at how quickly you can turn things around. Storms that lasted hours, days, or even weeks will shrink into a matter of minutes. Eventually, you'll get to a point where her dark Mood Glasses *don't even faze you.* You'll become the Man that is genuinely not intimidated by female emotions. No avoidance, no frustration, just a light-hearted confidence that *this too shall pass.*

A Man's Work

Part A: The Love Switch

If you want warmth, learn to spot the spark—and be the one who lights it. These exercises sharpen your awareness of what builds connection and what kills it. Gratitude, self-awareness, and small daily choices shift everything. Don't wait for her to change. Practice these, and you flip the Switch.

1) Switch Spotting

Instructions: Each day this week, write down in your notebook one moment your wife felt distant or warm. Write down what happened just before? What did you do? Then, write one small action that could've helped sparked connection (e.g., a hug, a joke). Reflect on how your actions—or lack thereof—affected her Switch? At the end of week, look back and track what helps or doesn't help shift her emotional state.

Purpose: This develops awareness of emotional dynamics and encourages proactive connection.

2) Best Character Traits

Instructions: Know your strengths. Write three traits you've lived out (e.g., "I'm steady—I keep my word"), plus two you want to grow. Ask three close people: "What are my best traits?" Reflect on how these can serve you in your life. Use them this week to lead with confidence.

Purpose: This reinforces your self-worth, helping you to meet her needs with freedom rather than desperation.

3) Gratitude Anchor

Instructions: Gratitude builds connection faster than logic or blame. Each morning, write three things in your notebook you're grateful for: one about you, one about her, one about your marriage. Be specific (e.g., "I'm grateful for her laugh when we watched that funny movie"). At night, reflect: Did that shift your actions? Share one with her by the end of the week.

Purpose: This fosters positive emotions which is necessary for you to have a magnetic presence.

Part B: The Mood Glasses

You don't need to fix her mood—you need to help lighten her load. These exercises help you see her world through her eyes, to create joy with intention, and to embody the man she trusts. It's not about faking peace; it's about becoming the one who brings it. Start small. Practice daily.

1) Mood Glasses Journal (Journaling Prompt)

Instructions: Her mood colors everything—and you can shift the shade. Recall a time she seemed dark or reactive. What did she say? How did you respond? What might she have felt underneath? Write one thing you could've done to lift her mood. Reflect on how this might have changed her glasses. Do this daily to master the art of brightening her emotional lens.

Purpose: This encourages reflection on missed opportunities to lighten her mood.

2) Positive Emotions Practice

Instructions: Pick three positive emotions you want more of in your marriage—things like joy, safety, trust. When did you last feel them with her? What sparked it? Write in your notebook for 15 minutes. Reflect on when you last feel these with her? What sparked them? Then plan one action to create each emotion this week. Follow through and watch how her energy responds. Remember, it's your superpower to shift her world. So, hone that power.

Purpose: This builds skills to create positive emotional states, enabling you to lighten her Mood Glasses.

3) Avatar: Who You Could Be

Instructions: Spend 20 minutes designing your ideal self—the calm, steady King. Name him. Describe how he walks, talks, leads in conflict. Now be him: 1) Speak as him in the mirror. 2) Order coffee as him. 3) Show up that way with friends. 4) Hold one boundary as him this week. Remember, you're not pretending—you're becoming.

Purpose: Creates a framework so your confident self can enforce boundaries, aligning with masculine structure. Recondition your nervous system and subconscious mind to act from a more powerful place.

Notes to Self

THE SIXTH LAW: NO FEAR

You might have come across the term 'the state of nature' before. It's a favourite of philosophers like Jean-Jacques Rousseau and John Locke, who used it to create origin stories about what human life was like before the creation of law and order. The most famous of these is Thomas Hobbes' state of nature, which describes life without any form of government as a war of "every man against every man," rendering human life "solitary, poor, nasty, brutish, and short." In Hobbes' state of nature there is pure equality, but it's an equality of vulnerability. Every individual can harm others and be harmed by them, creating an endless cycle of anxiety and conflict.

I'd like you to imagine yourself in this scenario. But not for a day or a year. Imagine that your entire life is like this. Furthermore, put yourself back in time, before things like firearms and other weapons were invented. The primal world. It's just you and your comparatively puny fists. In such a world, you cannot trust anyone, because in a world without rules, treachery is not only possible but sometimes prudent. Social ties are overshadowed by the constant fear that today's ally may be tomorrow's rival. In this arena, life is consumed by the grim realities of survival: securing food, defending oneself, and navigating the treacherous intentions of others. Fear governs all, as death by violence looms over everything.

No doubt you've imagined a scenario a little bit like this before—such as how you'd fare in a zombie apocalypse or in the hunger games—but let's be honest, survival mode wouldn't be very fun when you had to live it twenty-four-seven, year after year.

When you really sit down and imagine the toll it would take, you'd be right to thank God that you don't live in a world where you constantly feel threatened. Where you're not continually scanning your immediate surroundings for both real and imagined predators. In short, a world where a man can just be a man and more or less make his way through life unmolested by physical violence.

Thank God, indeed—but take another moment, and think what it might be like to live in the state of nature if you weren't 5'10" and weighed 200 pounds. That you couldn't bench press 150 pounds or punch a hole in the wall if you were really angry. In this second scenario, you're smaller, lighter, less strong and don't have much appetite for violence. Now, you're only 5'4" and weigh about 165 pounds. You're not used to bench pressing more than about 55 pounds and you're not particularly inclined to punching anything. In this scenario, survival in the state of nature looks much more precarious. Less assured. The world is suddenly filled with far more potential threats than when you were the average height and weight of the typical American male. But that's because you're now the typical height, weight, and strength of the average American woman.

Now, you can hopefully imagine at least some of what your partner feels even today, because the world looks very different to the average woman compared to the average man. You may not see the physical threats that still exist in the world, but that's because you don't feel threatened by them in the same way. Most women, and it is crucial you understand this, still feel acutely concerned for their physical safety on a regular basis—and that's not limited to dark alleys and scary-looking guys on the street. It can include men like their fathers, brothers, husbands, and older sons.

With that in mind, don't just limit yourself to thinking about the ways in which the world looks different to your partner. Think about the fact that you can look very different to her. That you can be part of the problem. Because when you're enraged, angry, or edgy, you don't feel like you're her husband anymore. Consciously or not, she now feels that you are a potential threat. Which, in essence, makes you a real threat. Because when you're angry, you're dangerous and she experiences that sense of danger. You may not feel like a threat, but that doesn't matter. Danger, like beauty, is in the eye of the beholder.

If you came across a bear in the wild, it wouldn't matter if the bear was thinking to itself that it wasn't going to attack you—you'd still be scared that it would. That's because you can't accurately predict the bear's behaviour since a) you're not a bear; b) you don't know what the bear is thinking; and c) you feel intrinsically vulnerable around something more powerful than you. But that's the point: when you're angry, you're the bear. You can make your partner feel extremely vulnerable and that should trouble you. Deeply. It should render you speechless. To think that the woman whom you love more than anyone in the world, whom you vowed to protect and cherish, should feel the exact opposite ought to be a wake-up call. It should hit you like a gut-punch.

It's Evolutionary, My Dear Watson

Men and women are very different. That's pretty obvious, but those differences have a long history. Some of this comes down to evolution, while other aspects are related to cultural and social changes over time. To help you understand the real and powerful dynamic that's at work whenever you get angry and she gets fearful, we need to dig a little deeper into these differences. This is necessary work. As the philosopher Søren Kierkegaard once wrote, "Life can only be understood looking backwards, but it has to be lived going forwards." This will help you do so.

At any point in history—though less so now—women needed a strong man to protect them from the dangers of the world. Remember, we have not always lived in air-conditioned condos; for most of human history, we lived in caves and huts. That was a deeply unsafe world. A woman could be high on the food chain, but she wasn't the highest, as there were predators abounding from saber-toothed tigers to cave bears. Rival groups and dangerous men posed substantial risks, ranging from abduction and rape to being used and abused as a reproductive resource. In fact, reproduction itself was a scary business. Thanks to biological vulnerabilities and environmental hazards, childbirth was one of the leading causes of death. Exacerbated by poor nutrition and frequent pregnancies, many women could be left physically weakened for long periods of time—to say nothing about life without painkillers and antibiotics. Physically taxing domestic tasks, such as grinding grain or carrying water, led to chronic injuries, and the lack of hygiene left women at high risk of infection, especially during menstruation and childbirth. In short, life could be pretty bad for a prehistoric or ancient woman.

Given the danger that most men posed to women, the best solution (though by no means perfect) was to team up with one, inviting that dangerous, violent man into her life: harnessing his power in the service of her own protection. In essence, to become man and wife. But in order for this to work, for her to feel safe, the woman needed to know that the man's aggression would only be directed outward, toward defending her, rather than inward, toward harming her. But as we all know, tamed lions are still lions. Dormant volcanoes can still erupt. When the lion roars or the volcano rumbles, those who are paying attention keep their distance. So, too, with husbands and wives. The instinct to avoid a husband or partner's harm runs deep—like, hundreds of thousands of years deep. A woman would rather be safe than sorry, preferring to over-protect herself than delay and risk getting hurt. As mentioned, this has a long evolutionary history, but it's not like violence against women is limited to the distant past either.

Even in developed nations, as recently as our grandparents' generation, wife-beating was not uncommon. It took until the 1970s in most developed countries for laws against domestic violence to be enforced with any kind of rigor. It's no surprise, therefore, that even as late as 1963 the film *From Russia with Love* features James Bond violently slapping a woman—as if it was a positive thing. Rewatching the film, I was reminded that our contemporary sensibilities around not harming women are *very* new. Don't get me wrong, I'm glad that we've progressed this far, but we still have a long way to go. It's important to remember that for virtually 99.9% of human history, men being violent toward their wives was normalized across cultures. In much of the world, it is still normal to this day. Women are deeply, instinctively aware of this historical reality, even if it sometimes goes unspoken. That's why it's so important that men learn about this, lest we continue perpetuating the cycle in our own marriages.

Alarm Bells

So the next time you get into an argument with your partner—when you raise your voice, punch a hole in the wall (as I've done), throw something across the room, or even just have an edge of annoyance in your voice—recognize that you're triggering her survival instincts. That the part of her brain that has been shaped by evolution will be ringing its alarm bells. It will be telling her that she's now alone with someone who's likely 60-70 pounds heavier than her and far more equipped for violence. She will immediately feel the evolutionary reality of the situation—she is trapped alone with a big, angry predator.

From that place of fear, she's going to respond in one of a few ways. She might try to comply with you, saying and doing whatever she thinks will make you happy so the threat will go away. She might try to escape—leave the room, the house, or even seek refuge with her parents or friends. Or she might try to respond in kind. She'll tap into her own masculine aggression, meeting you head on. If she picks fight rather than flight, she runs the risk of escalating and magnifying your own aggressiveness. But no matter which response she chooses, you'll notice that none of these scenarios resolve whatever was causing the quarrel in the first place. If she placates you, it's just papering over the problem. Likewise, if she hides from you, the problem doesn't go with her—it will linger on and fester, like an open wound. The last option doesn't work either for obvious reasons, not least because the chance of physical or psychological harm increases as the fight intensifies.

If you're in a negative situation and you notice any (or all) of these responses—whether it's compliance that feels forced, withdrawal from you, or an escalation of aggression—understand that they all stem from her feeling unsafe. It's not about the surface-level disagreement. It's about her survival system kicking in because, on some level, she's perceiving you as a threat. The fact that she even feels that way about you is bad news, but the good news is that you can do something positive about this. Something that changes the dynamic and helps your wife to feel safe around you again.

Men Live on Mars

We've heard it said many times that men are from Mars and women are from Venus. It might be more accurately said that men and women, while sharing the same planet, are an entirely different species—that's how differently we perceive reality. If most women are hardwired to sense physical threats in their surroundings, most men don't give it a second thought. At least, not on a regular basis. If you ask the average man, "When was the last time you were afraid?" most men will respond that they don't really remember. Likewise, if you get more specific and ask about the last time they were afraid for their physical safety, they'll probably answer that it was a long time ago. You might hear responses like, "Maybe like 10 years ago, or that time outside of the bar, or the time where I was in combat." But even then, I've coached *actual combat veterans* who couldn't remember the last time they felt physically unsafe. For many guys, they have to go back to their childhood or teenage years—back to when they weren't at the top of the food chain. It's not that men can't or shouldn't feel concerned for their safety. Rather, it's because we're so used to being so high on the survival ladder. Men are predators, they're not very accustomed to thinking like prey.

Now, if you ask the average woman when the last time she was afraid for her physical safety, she's going to say, "Yesterday. Last week. This morning." That's because the world that women inhabit is full of potential threats and they have a sixth-sense for it. A sense that we don't have—at least, not to the same degree. Not to the same sensitivity. When a man walks to his car at night, he won't notice the other males around—unless there's a menacing group of them. That's when he might be on his guard, but it probably won't stop him from walking to his car. But when the average woman walks to her car at night, or even into the next aisle in Walmart, she's far more likely to notice every man there. She'll be acutely aware of who could be dangerous. The men that are invisible to you are highly visible to her.

Don't get me wrong. There's plenty of women in the world who are both strong and courageous. My own wife is one of those. But on average, the female experience is different to that of males. Fueled by testosterone, men have a narrow, predator-like focus. We're hardwired for the hunt, the kill. Women, by contrast, have diffuse awareness. Like prey animals, they're aware of multiple things at the same time; they can multitask, scanning their surroundings for a multitude of signals as they go about their daily business. As foreign as a woman's experience may feel to you as a man, as a husband you have to learn to empathize with your wife's heightened sensitivity to such threats. That said, I'm not really talking about the threat that other men pose to her (important as that may be). I'm talking about the threat that you pose to her.

Control Your Anger

No one likes to feel trapped, especially women. Imagine, therefore, that you're alone together at home. You're having a disagreement and there's an edge in your voice. You might not think anything of it, because hurting your wife has never crossed your mind—but it will cross her mind. Perhaps not on a conscious level—she might be 100% certain that you would never hurt her—but as much as she might *think* you're safe, she won't *feel* safe. That's because she's trapped in a house with an angry man who's both heavier, stronger and more capable of violence than her. Her brain knows its evolutionary history and will be sending her body warning signals. Her autonomic nervous system will kick into overdrive, signalling the adrenal glands to release both adrenaline and cortisol. Her heart rate and blood pressure will increase, her muscles will tense and her senses—particularly her sight and hearing—will become hyper-alert. Her body has switched into survival mode. And all this can happen without either of you really noticing. But if you were to look at her behaviour, posture, and mood, you'll notice what's happening.

But that's not usually what happens. Since men don't experience what women do, we often misread both the situation and ourselves. We think that our anger expresses our passion and, in a way, how much we care. After all, we wouldn't be getting angry unless we thought it was about something important. As such, we tend to see our anger as a development or an escalation of an existing situation—namely an argument—rather than as a transformation of one situation into another. But for her, you're no longer arguing. Now, you're threatening and this is a different situation altogether. That's why she might say something like "I can't have this conversation any more" and retreat to her room—but also why we might follow or chase her. It's why we open the door and continue the fight, because we think we're doing the right thing. That we're going to settle this so that we don't go to bed angry. But again, that's not how your wife sees (or feels) the situation. Now the predator is stalking her, trying to corner and trap her even in her place of refuge.

It's amazing how wrong men can get this—including me. Before I learned how to recognise the signs of my wife's growing sense of danger, I would try to keep arguing until the argument was over. That's not because I love arguing, I don't. I simply wanted to restore order. To right wrongs and settle things. I wanted to bring some harmony back into our lives—but it turned out that I was accomplishing the exact opposite. For example, one time during an argument Whitney retreated to our bedroom and locked the door. She didn't want to continue the 'conversation', but like so many men, I did. I thought we needed to resolve things then and there to avoid resentment building up. In short, I wanted her to act like a grownup, not like a little kid hiding in her bedroom—so I did something stupid. I picked the lock, neglecting the fact that this would make her feel vulnerable and trapped. Here I was, bigger and stronger than her, acting just like an actual predator. My actions were sending the kind of message that says "You're not safe here. No matter where you go, I can get to you." This was obviously not my intention. I even thought she might be mildly impressed: first, that I could pick the lock, and second that I was so committed to resolving the conflict between us. Needless to say, she wasn't.

Stupid as that was, most men don't realize the impact our anger can have because we're not taught about it. Yes, we know that we're not meant to get angry—grace under pressure and all that, but we're not told why. At least, not when it comes to women. It's not explained to us in a comprehensive way. One that enables us to understand how she sees the world through her own eyes—and to see ourselves as they see us. The good thing is that there isn't actually that much to teach. That's because it's pretty simple. Your primary task is to avoid being angry with your wife. This will be beneficial for you, because it lowers the risks of heart disease and high blood pressure, reduces stress and anxiety, and improves your self-control and decision making skills. But more importantly, it will benefit your wife. It will provide her with the kind of safety, security and comfort that she needs in order to have a thriving marriage.

If you aren't sure this applies to you, talk to your wife about it. *Ask her if your anger has ever made her feel vulnerable, unsafe or threatened.* You'll probably get one of two answers. The most common response is, "Well, yeah, obviously. How could you not know that? Of course I'm afraid of you when you're angry." The second answer might be more like this, "You know what? I never really thought about it that consciously. But yeah, totally. I never thought you would hit me, but that doesn't mean I wasn't scared. In fact, I've definitely been afraid of you when you're angry." Whichever response you get, you'll find that her answer will help make sense of a lot of her behaviour—be that her compliance, avoidance, or counter-aggression.

This realization—that your wife has, on many occasions, been afraid for her safety around you—should be a gut-punch for you.

It certainly was for me. Because I *never* wanted Whitney to feel afraid of me. I wanted to be her protector. Realizing how often I was the opposite was a serious wake-up call.

As I said, the big takeaway is that you can't unleash your anger on your wife. Not at her. Not around her. You may have legitimate reasons to be angry, but like a dam that holds back the waters, you need to learn the appropriate times and places to open those floodgates. The middle of an argument is not the right time. But if the pressure is too much to bear, ask her if it's okay for you to do a controlled outburst. Say something like "Hey, I'm feeling really pissed off right now. Can I express some of this anger to you?" Or "Look, I'm not in a good place right now. Can I just vent for a minute?" If you get that permission first, then it's a safe space to express your anger. But she needs to know that you're not going to direct that anger at her. You also need to ensure that you're capable of walking away before your anger gets the better of you. But that's the thing: *you can walk away.* Instead of entering into the Storm, you can be The Lighthouse, even if that means shining your light somewhere else. If you need to, call a time-out. Go for a walk. Have a shower. Listen to some music. Clear your head a bit. Let your heart settle down. That's not a sign of weakness. It's a sign of strength. It's you doing your marital duty, which is to love your wife, not to scare her.

The more you understand how your anger impacts your partner, the more you'll look back on the history of your relationship and see the damage that it's done. This alone should provide you with ample motivation to be a different man. A better man. Because in the end, the mission of every marriage is the same: to love and be loved—and that won't happen if your anger makes her afraid of you. But as it says in 1 John 4:18, "Perfect love casts out all fear."

Unfortunately, Nobody Is Perfect

Controlling your anger is one thing. Controlling yourself so that you don't get angry in the first place is another. But I can assure you that practice makes you better, even if it doesn't make you perfect. The key thing is to always try to keep your wife's need for safety in mind. Even in the heat of the moment, when you're really upset, look at your wife and learn to really see her—her welfare, her security, her safety. See the impact that you're having on her behaviour. Watch her body language. Remember that this is high-stakes stuff. You took a solemn, holy vow when you married this woman that you would always love and cherish her—even when you're really, really pissed off.

But, of course, nobody is perfect. Despite years of practice and massive progress, I still make mistakes. Just recently, my wife and I were driving back from a date and we got into a minor argument. We live well outside the city, so there was still some distance to drive. It wasn't a serious fight, but it got tense. Despite the fact that I know better, I spoke to her in an annoyed, edgy tone. Fortunately, I caught myself before things spiralled. When I did, I turned to Whitney and asked if she was feeling afraid of me—and her response startled me. "Yeah, of course, I am! We're in the middle of nowhere, there are no other cars on the road, I'm trapped alone with you, and we don't even have cell reception. Of course, I'm afraid!" Unlike her, I hadn't paid much attention to our surroundings: things like the dark, empty road and the absence of cell reception. To me, they'd been either invisible or irrelevant. But to her, those factors signalled danger. Her survival instincts were warning her that if this goes bad and he becomes violent, there's nothing she can do to stop him. This felt true to her despite the fact that she's a trained jiu-jitsu competitor. She knows how to fight and has been in hundreds if not thousands of matches. So trust me when I say that she's no wallflower. But again, facts don't change feelings. My anger made her feel acutely aware of her vulnerability—and none of this would have occurred to me unless I'd stopped, calmed down, and asked her how she was feeling. Once that had happened, I was able to apologize and we de-escalated the situation. Rather than ruining the date, we saved it.

If you find yourself in a similar situation, don't hesitate to check how she's feeling. You can ask her in a calm, caring manner whether your anger is making her afraid. Just make her aware that *you're* aware. That you won't let it escalate. That you can see how your anger is impacting her and that you're sorry—and that if she ever feels uncomfortable around you she can tell you and you'll respect that. Do this and be sure to follow through, even if it disrupts things. Even if it means that the next time you have an argument you need to pause the conversation, go to separate rooms, and wait until you've both calmed down—even if it's the next day. Contrary to the popular saying, it is absolutely OK to sometimes let the sun go down on your anger. By doing this, you'll be giving her something valuable. Namely, the gift of acknowledgment. You'll be demonstrating to her that you get it. That you get her and that you get yourself too.

In time, this gift will keep on giving. It will help transform you and your marriage. It will ensure that your wife always feels safe around you—which is essential if she's also going to feel not just safe, but seen, supported and special as well.

A Man's Work

Unchecked anger wounds everyone. These exercises will help you master it—not suppress it. You'll trace its roots, break generational patterns, and build new instincts. Each reflection is a step toward becoming the man who protects, not provokes. Don't fear the fire—face it. That's how you learn to carry it well.

1) Anger Triggers

Instructions: You're her protector, not a predator. But she needs to feel that, always. So write in your notebook about the last time you got angry. What sparked it? What did you do? How did she react? Now dig deeper—what old wound (e.g., shame, rejection) was behind it? Then write one thing you'll try next time to pause the rage. Do this after each flare-up.

Purpose: This helps uncover anger triggers and builds strategies to stay calm.

2) The Mother Wound

Instructions: Your anger has roots. Spend 20 minutes writing about your mother's impact—two parts: Harmful (e.g., criticism) and Missing (e.g., warmth). Even if you think she's a saint, stick with this exercise. Try to recall vivid moments. What patterns did you bring into your marriage (like approval-seeking)? This isn't blame—it's clarity. Keep this private and revisit it to track your progress.

Purpose: This identifies maternal influences on emotional reactivity, supporting anger control.

3) Breathwork (4-6-8 Method)

Instructions: When anger rises, breathe it down. In a quiet spot, inhale through your nose for 4 seconds. Hold for 6, picture that raging bear inside of you settling. Exhale through your mouth for 8. Repeat 6–8 rounds daily or when you feel the edge. This calms your body—and keeps her safe.

Purpose: This provides a tool to manage anger in real-time, ensuring safety.

Notes to Self

THE SEVENTH LAW: SHE NEEDS TO FEEL SEEN, SPECIAL, AND SUPPORTED

How much is a twenty dollar bill worth? You might think it's worth exactly that, twenty dollars. But think for a moment what it actually is. It's made from 75% cotton and 25% linen. There are some tiny red and blue synthetic fibers embedded into the fabric to help deter counterfeiting, and each note has security features like color-shifting ink and a watermark—but the individual components are virtually worthless. It only costs seventeen cents to make one, even though you can purchase twenty dollars worth of goods and services with it. The key thing about the bill is that we trust it. We feel safe using it. So long as that remains the case, a twenty dollar bill is worth twenty dollars. But what if you woke up one day and forgot to check the news. Perhaps there's been a terrible natural disaster or an apocalyptic financial collapse and for whatever reason, most people aren't interested in dollar bills anymore. You go to the store, but nobody wants to accept your money—though they're interested in trading for survival goods. You try to buy a coffee, but they refuse your twenty dollar bill. You're still not sure what's going on and why your money now seems worthless, but it wouldn't take more than a few transactions for you to no longer trust the value of it. Soon, money wouldn't feel safe to you. It wouldn't feel secure. In turn, you wouldn't feel as safe and secure either, both physically and emotionally.

Despite the fact that you've trusted in money until now and regardless of the fact that you've had thousands of successful transactions until this moment, money no longer represents safety and without that, who knows what you'll do. If you're the confrontational type, maybe at the next store you lose your temper. You shout and threaten them with violence—accept my twenty dollar bill or else! But perhaps you're more passive than that. You shut down and try to hide from the problem. You go without your coffee, you forget about this and that purchase, hoping that the problem goes away. But in either case, your attitude towards money will have shifted. The experience will have changed you and with it, your outlook, attitudes and actions. That's because money is central to modern life and without the sense of safety and security that it provides, it's virtually impossible to live a normal life, let alone flourish.

What's true of money is also true for marriage. It represents safety at a fundamental level. For most men, this safety feels bedrock. It's a firm foundation and it would take an earthquake to shift it. For most women, however, the sense of safety is more like a boat. It could sail the world's oceans, but even small waves can rock it. The boat may be entirely seaworthy and has plenty of life jackets aboard, but a single wave—let alone a large swell or storm—can be enough to make one feel unsafe. Indeed, even mild rocking can make a person feel terribly seasick. At its best, nothing beats sailing and that's why people crave the open ocean, but to return to marriage, the sense of safety it provides a woman is far more volatile than the bedrock sense of safety that a man gets from marriage. For example, something that may be triggering for a wife may not even register on her husband's radar, let alone make him feel unsafe or insecure in his marriage—but as you know, a marriage isn't measured by how well couples handle their similarities, it's measured by how well they navigate their differences.

That's why this chapter is all about understanding why your wife often feels unsafe and what you can do about it. Naturally, it's a complement to what we've already covered, such as the importance of being The Lighthouse, understanding her Love Switch and Mood Glasses, as well as not making her feel physically unsafe—but this chapter delves into her deeper emotions. It explains why she's feeling emotionally unsafe in a variety of situations and just as importantly, what you can do to quickly restore her sense of safety—not merely because it helps her to feel happy again in the short term, but because it's key to being happily married in the long run too. *Use this chapter as your resource to interpret her emotions when you just can't figure out why the hell she seems so upset.*

When a Spade is Not a Spade

A woman's emotions often seem unfathomable to a man. To make matters worse, not only do women experience things very differently than men, they often articulate their experiences very differently too. Men are usually more blunt. More direct. If a man has something he needs to communicate, he'll fire at will. He may try to sugarcoat it a bit depending on who he's talking to, but there's a clear connection between what he's saying and how he's feeling. In essence, he means what he says. His words aren't hiding any hidden depths. For example, imagine two guys are roommates: one is tidy, the other isn't. The tidy one comes home and finds the kitchen is a mess. He'll say to the other guy, "Dude, the kitchen is a mess. Every day when I get home I have to clean up after you before I can start cooking. That's annoying. Please clean up after yourself." Boom. Done. Whether the messy roommate actually cleans up after himself is another matter, but as far as the conversation went, everything was put on the table—so to speak. The problem was stated and the opportunity to resolve it was presented. There were no hidden messages, no subtle cues. There was absolutely no guesswork required.

As you might guess, the situation is completely different when these two roommates are in fact husband and wife. Let's say that your wife is the tidy one and you're the messy one—even if you're not actually that messy... She comes home and sees a mess, but instead of telling you straight up that you need to do the dishes, she brings up something from six weeks or six months ago. You don't get why she's bringing this up now, but it doesn't seem fair, relevant or accurate. You wonder what's going on? What's this all about? It's not that she isn't upset about the mess, she is; but from a male perspective she's not addressing the situation head on. She's indirectly addressing the facts by directly addressing her feelings—but for her, the way she feels about the mess is connected to the way she felt about something else, but that connection isn't directly communicated to you. And that's why you're left scratching your head.

Obviously, this situation is not ideal. What Winston Churchill once said of Stalin, you've no doubt said about your own wife—that she's like a riddle wrapped in a mystery that's hidden inside an enigma. But Churchill also said that there was a key to figuring out Stalin, which required understanding Russia's national interest. It wasn't a perfect solution, but it was a helpful way of simplifying a mysterious situation—a similar approach can help you understand your wife. To do this, we need to understand what a woman actually *needs* from her marriage. Indeed, what every wife wants from her husband. As you might have guessed, the answer can be boiled down to safety—but it's more than that. For a wife to feel safe in her marriage, she needs to feel Seen, Special, and Supported. If she's not feeling any or all of these things, she'll respond in ways that will mystify, upset, or madden you. Of course, she's not likely going to come right out and say that she's feeling unseen, unspecial, and/or unsupported, which means you have to learn to figure out what's bothering her.

Seen, Special, Supported

Men and women both have masculine and feminine traits, not least because every human has testosterone, estrogen and progesterone hormones. But as we've already discussed, men have more testosterone on average than women, just as females have more estrogen and progesterone on average than males. For many women, this equates to possessing (or having the capacity to construct) a masculine protective shell, as well as a softer, more nurturing, feminine core—and just as every seed was made to sprout, so too her core wants to be uncovered. A wife wants to share her inner-self with her husband, just as a river wants to reach the sea. But for this to happen, she needs to feel safe. Not just physically, but emotionally. And not just once, but (almost) always. As such it's worth recapping just a little bit why emotional-physical safety is so important for women.

As we discussed in the last chapter, the world is much less safe for women than it is for men. That is one of the reasons why, in evolutionary terms, women have sought the protection of a man. The best way for most women to do this, historically, has been to marry one. Though the 21st century is much safer than the 16th century (or 200,000 years ago for that matter), contemporary life still poses threats for women, besides the evolutionary instinct to partner with a protector-male is hardwired into her psyche. For that reason, a woman needs to know that she is safe both *with* her man, but also *from* him: that he'll protect her from the sabertooth tiger and the bandits, but also from himself—that his physical strength won't ever be used against her.

For her to know all these things, she'll assess you, consciously or not, on a regular basis in order to reassure herself that you're still up to the job. She'll look at how you handle your own stressful emotions and crises as well as hers—often stress-testing you to check for potential weaknesses. So the next time there's a bump in the night and somebody needs to check it out, or the next time someone cuts in front of you in traffic and you're tempted to unleash some road rage, remember that you're being observed. She's looking for your emotional equanimity. To see if you keep your cool. It's not that she *wants* to find any shortcomings, but again, for her safety is paramount, so she feels the need to know. Likewise, she'll assess how well you protect her and any children you have—like whether you've fixed the lock on the door or ensured the gas tank isn't left empty—because these signal to her whether or not you take her security seriously. Failure to do these things signals danger. It indicates a lack of safety and protection. For a man, many of these things aren't practical concerns, let alone existential dangers—but this isn't about you. It's not about how you see the world. It's about how your wife sees it. How she feels about it. And frankly, it does matter, because you have to live with her.

Your wife needs to feel seen, special, and supported on a continual basis in order to feel safe enough to let down her guard around you. She needs this in order to let her kind, nurturing, feminine inner-self shine. If she doesn't feel that way, the guards come back up—be that in the form of fight or flight, being cold or distant, or something else entirely. That's because it's impossible for her to feel entirely safe if she feels emotionally unsafe. These are linked, like components in an electrical circuit. For the light to shine, all the components need to be connected, otherwise the current won't flow. To help visualise this, take a look below.

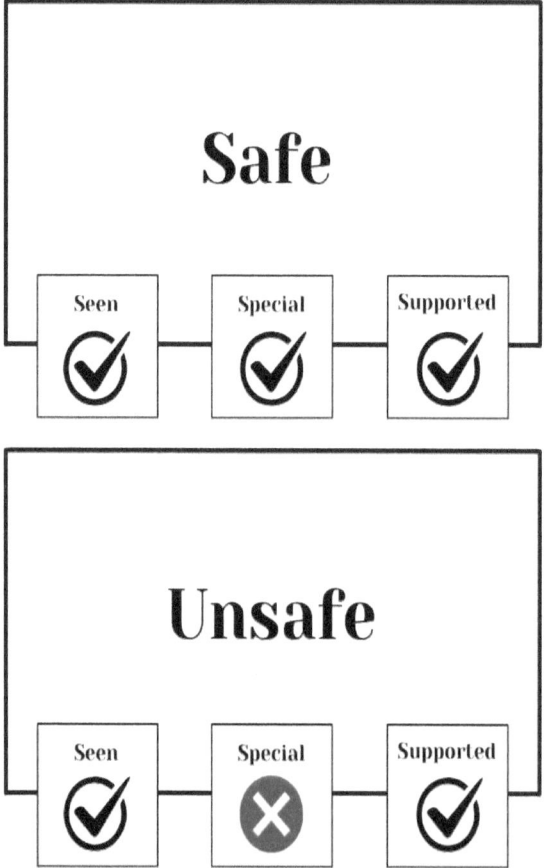

For her to feel safe, all three boxes need to be ticked. If she's acting in a manner that suggests she's not feeling safe, it's most likely because the tick mark in one or more of these boxes has just become an X. For example, if she's complaining that you don't get her and she keeps revisiting the same issue over and over again—perhaps it's about a comment you made at a dinner party—it's likely she doesn't feel seen. She doesn't feel like you understand her or know what's going on inside of her. Likewise, if she's making a big deal about you complimenting another woman, it's probably because she doesn't feel special. She's not feeling like she's the center of your world or that you think she's uniquely beautiful. And lastly, if she's being hypercritical about a pair of dirty boxers you left on the bedroom floor, it's probably because she's feeling unsupported. She may be feeling overwhelmed by the number of personal, professional, or domestic matters that she's currently juggling and rather than helping her, she thinks you're oblivious to the demands she's facing. These are just a few examples, and they're not particularly complicated ones—we'll cover others in more detail later—but it's important that you understand this. That you understand her. And that your wife sees that you do. That she feels it. Otherwise, you'll be stuck fighting the smoke rather than the fire. It'll be symptoms, not causes.

Technically speaking, a more accurate diagram would have circles rather than boxes, with each of the circles overlapping, because feeling seen, special, and supported are often overlapping issues. They're deeply interconnected. But let's keep them in separate boxes for simplicity's sake. Because the next time your wife is acting upset—when she's distant, cold, confrontational, or just not feeling right—you'll need to ask yourself whether she's feeling unseen, unspecial, or unsupported? You'll need to discern which of these three is the primary reason she's feeling unsafe right now. But if you're really not sure, you can do worse than simply checking in with her. Ask her meaningful questions in a caring, supportive manner. Something like, "Hey, I can see that this is stressful and I want to help. It's important to me that you feel I get it. Would it help if I _____?" You can insert something into the blank easily enough and pair it with some kind of concrete action—like giving her a rest, taking her out for a meal, or whatever else might lift her up and make her feel loved. Even if you don't quite hit the nail on the head, she will feel an improvement. She will see that you are making an effort to understand her and to love her. And this, husbands, will go a long way.

I get that the idea of ensuring that your wife continually feels seen, special, and supported sounds like a lot of work. At first, it might indeed be hard yards. But as with the Love Switch and the Mood Glasses, it doesn't take that much to improve your wife's emotional state. Soon, you'll get the hang of it. But also, it's important to remember that *you are married to her.* You will have made promises on your wedding day to love your wife for better and for worse, which includes when it's annoying or inconvenient. When it seems like a lot of work. This includes when it feels like it's just you making all the effort. But trust me on this one, when you learn to love your wife in such a way that she always feels safe—because she feels seen, special, and supported—the respect and appreciation that you get back will blow your mind. As we've all heard, and there is truth to it, happy wife, happy life.

Seen

When it comes to ensuring that your wife feels seen by you, it's important to remember that *knowing* something and *feeling* it are two different things. Your facts aren't going to change her feelings. That's because this isn't head-stuff: it's heart-stuff. For her to feel seen—that she's understood, that you get it and get her—she may need to run through something multiple times or bring in seemingly unrelated examples. Let her. It's not because she's being difficult or crazy (or at least not on purpose). It's because she doesn't feel fully understood yet. Besides, she'll keep at this until she does feel understood, so you might as well go all in too, even if it means temporarily drowning in a sea of unnecessary details. As they say in England, "In for a penny, in for a pound."

A large part of making her feel understood is simply *recognizing her fears.* Remember that one. It will serve you well. Take this example: you're driving, and the car makes a small noise.

You know it's nothing serious, but she fixates on it, asking for explanations and reassurance. She gets really worked up about it. Instead of jumping straight into fact-mode, explaining the car's design and the engine's construction—in essence, telling her why she shouldn't worry—focus instead on understanding her fear. She needs to feel that you acknowledge and validate her emotions. In this scenario, she's not feeling seen—and therefore safe—because you aren't addressing her feeling of fear. You may think that you're addressing her fears vis-a-vis the car's reliability (AKA, the facts) but that's not the same as addressing her feelings. What matters is this: she feels that *you understand that she's afraid.* She needs to know that her protector *recognizes how big the threat is* (and more accurately how big it *feels* to her) and that you care enough to empathize with her emotions.

There's more than one way to do this, but you could try something like putting your hand on her knee or arm and saying, "Hey, it's okay. I get that you're worried about the car, because you are worried that we might break down and not get to the hotel in time, which would be *brutal.* I get that. But I've got it covered. The car is not going to break down and we are definitely going to be at the hotel on time." The thing to remember is that it's more important for her to feel that you understand how *serious something seems to her* than it is for her to understand your solution. If you grasp that she perceives the tiny rattle in the car as a threatening event and you show her *you get how big it feels to her,* her fear will start to fade. But if you focus solely on explaining the mechanics of the car, her fear will linger, unaddressed.

This same principle applies to understanding her needs. She will have needs that might seem trivial or unimportant to you, but it's crucial to understand *why* they matter to her. Often, it's more important for her to feel that you understand her needs than for you to actually address them. For example, if she insists that you lock the door every single time you step out, even if it's just for three minutes, what she truly wants is for you to understand why that's important to her. Once she feels understood, once you recognize her fear that bad guys could get in AT ANY MOMENT

AND THE WHOLE WORLD COULD END, she may not even care about the action itself. It's not really about the door—it's about you recognizing her fear and showing her that you get it. Don't offer her solutions, offer her solidarity.

Another part of making her feel seen is emotional connection. She's going to share details—lots of details—about her friendships, work, or whatever's happening in her life. She needs you to share details back. If she asks how your day went and you respond with, "Good," that's enough for you—but it's not enough for her. You don't have to match the level of detail she might share with her girlfriends, obviously, but offering two or three sentences about something that went right, went wrong, or stood out will go a long way in helping her feel connected to you emotionally. That's because she needs to feel that she's talking *with* you, not *to* you. And to be honest, that's not so much to ask. But I get that it may seem like another task to do at the end of a long day, but the good news is that the more you give her that sense of being understood, the less she'll need it in the future. That goes for *everything* in this book.

If you commit to this upfront—putting in extra effort to make her feel understood over the next one, two, or three months—you'll find that the level of effort required later will drop dramatically. Of course, you don't want to spend forever listening to her stressed-out stream of consciousness. Men have limits, and it's okay to tell her that at some point. But until she feels that you value her enough to understand her, you need to put in the time. But once she feels that you genuinely want to understand her, she'll trust that you're willing to take the necessary time to do so—*and that's precisely when she'll need less reassurance.* But again, this is worth doing even without this reward because you love your wife—and part of loving her is making sure that she feels loved by you. Ensuring this happens is worth the effort and will pay big dividends later.

Special

Simply put, your wife needs to feel like you are pleased with her. Alison Armstrong really helped me to understand this, particularly that it's not enough for a woman to feel like she's a great wife and mother, but more importantly, that *you* think she's a great wife and mom. This is essential, especially because women develop and grow differently from men. Whereas men tend to grow from pressure, women tend to grow through praise. If you nurture her strengths and recognize what she's good at, she will grow in those areas and branch out to others, becoming even better. Feeling like a good wife or a good mom is what enables her to be a good wife and mom. For men, the opposite is often true—we often become better husbands and fathers when we recognize our shortcomings and feel driven to improve on them. It's when I know that I'm falling short that I find the motivation to grow and go the extra mile. But women are built differently. If a woman feels bad about herself as a wife or mom, she's likely to withdraw from those areas that make her feel inadequate.

To that end, your wife needs to feel like she's not just a great wife and mom but also that you actively see her that way and communicate it to her. This affirmation will help her improve in those roles and carry that confidence into other areas of her life. Likewise, she needs to feel uniquely special—whether that's uniquely beautiful, smart, hardworking or whatever else it is that her identity is centered around. Every woman is different in what matters most to them. For some, intelligence may not be central, and while she'll appreciate efforts to make her feel smart, it won't resonate as deeply. Instead, it may be her creativity, organizing, or nurturing abilities. The key is to focus on what truly matters to her and validate it. To celebrate it. Because the more you invest in affirming her strengths, the more special you'll make her feel. And the more than happens, the stronger your connection will become.

But it's not just about affirming her strengths. Your wife needs to feel like she's the most important woman on earth to you. This includes being prioritized above your mom and even your kids. The caveat with the kids is that while she knows you probably have a special love for your son or daughter—a love that's different and perhaps even stronger than your love for her—she still needs to feel like she is the most important woman in your life. This is a real priority, because women can get jealous about the time or attention you give to your children, especially daughters. While this might seem selfish or narcissistic, it's actually rooted in her deep-seated need for safety. If she feels she's not that special to you, her subconscious interprets it as a lack of protection—"He won't protect me from the saber-tooth tiger." You know that's not true, but that won't change her feelings.

So you need to balance your attention. By all means, spend as much time with your kids as you think is right. Obviously. Call your daughter beautiful as often as you'd like—your wife wants you to do that—but also ensure you're giving your wife the attention and compliments she needs. This will help her feel secure and unthreatened by the love and affection you show others, even if she encourages you to show it. Even when it comes to helping others, like your mom, make sure your wife still feels like the priority in your overall life, even if she isn't in that moment. If she feels secure in being the most important woman in your life, she'll encourage you to help your mom or others. But if she feels like your mom comes first, she may create conflict between you and your mom, which benefits no one. When you prioritize her, she'll be proud to have a husband who does so much for others, whether it's for family, friends, or neighbors.

And lastly, your wife needs to feel like she's the only woman you have eyes for. I know that it's pretty common for men to follow models on Instagram, subscribe to OnlyFans, or put up pictures of attractive women in the man cave or garage—but even if a woman says she's okay with it, it's still deeply damaging to her sense of security and specialness. Many of my clients' wives insisted they weren't bothered by this—but once the relationship heals, safety returns, and real emotional connection is rebuilt, they often admit: *it always hurt, they just didn't feel safe enough to say so.* This is true for all women, even if they claim otherwise. So, as a basic rule of thumb: don't check out other women in front of your wife. Don't follow models on social media, and don't display sexy pictures of other women in your home or office. She needs to know that she's your priority, especially in relation to other women. That you feel privileged to be with her. That you're thrilled by her, no less than when you first started dating. Do this, and she will feel like she's the most special woman in the world. And she'll treat you like the man who makes her feel that way deserves.

Supported

Lastly, to feel supported, your wife needs to feel like you'll always fend for her. Some of this is material in nature. It's financial. It's the sense that you will work to ensure that her worldly needs are met. But that's not the whole picture. A lot of it has to do with physical and emotional matters. First, she needs to know that you'll protect her and care for her. That she'll always be safe. But also that you'll always be there to take her side and back her up in social situations, regardless of whether that's with loved ones or strangers. She needs to know that you'll be there to support her and take things off her plate when she's stressed or burnt out. She wants to feel reassured that her white knight is always ready to help shoulder some of her responsibilities, because every woman needs to occasionally relax and get away from it all—if only for twenty minutes on a Tuesday night! In short, your wife needs to feel that you're there for her, no matter what.

Obviously, this is no easy task. At least, not at first. Especially if the goal is to be proactive about it, rather than reactive—because as helpful as it is to know how to put all the pieces back together again, it's better if you can keep them from falling apart in the first place. Indeed, if you can understand her needs deeply enough that you can anticipate and address them before she even asks, it goes a very long way. But don't worry, because figuring this out isn't as hard as it sounds. You can begin just by looking around the house. What's going on? Are there jobs that need doing? Is there a mess to be cleaned up? Is your wife doing something that you could do instead? Likewise, you can look ahead. What needs to be done tomorrow? This week? Can you get a start on it now? Because if you can, you'll lighten your wife's load and this will mean a lot to her. For instance, instead of just recognizing that your wife is struggling to get the kids ready for school in the morning and stepping in to make breakfast, imagine you made their lunches the night before. You did this because you noticed she's got a busy week with lots of work, social obligations, and other stressors, so you took care of the lunches in advance. When she wakes up and sees that done, she feels incredibly supported and safe. This way, instead of being a good errand boy that does what she asks (and then you end up feeling like an employee) you take charge, take over, be proactive, and lead the relationship from a place of service.

So, too, you can do more than lighten her load. You can give her a break, becoming her source of peace. You want her to view you as her *provider* of peace, not as someone she has to *escape* to find peace. As I've said before, this is your superpower. And I have a cheat code for you. The next time you can sense your wife is stressed, overwhelmed, rude, impatient with the kids, etc. try this: send her to her bedroom with a glass of wine and tell her to watch an episode of that crappy TV show that you hate (and she loves). Tell her no one is going to disturb her for 45 or 90 minutes. You won't ask her where the kids' backpacks are, the kids won't ask her where their iPads are… You're going to protect her peace. This alone constitutes a mini-vacation and she'll feel immensely supported: all because you demonstrated that you've got her back. That you know what she needs, even if it's just a moment of calm in a sea of stress.

Even better, not only will she feel supported and therefore safe, her level of attraction to you will deepen. And most importantly, and this is why it is a cheat code, *the woman who comes out of the room will not be the same woman who went in*. She will come out of the bedroom soft, nurturing, and appreciative—her feminine core will shine more brightly. Just watch how this works. I've had *many* clients in sexless marriages get laid the *very first time* they do this. I'm not saying that's going to happen for you. But I am saying *this is a cheatcode*. And what makes it even better (again, like everything in this book) is that when she knows you are the kind of man that will do this for her when she needs it… will make her need it less over time.

But the bottom line is this: if she needs you, you're there. If you can anticipate her needs and fulfill them before she even asks you, all the better—and trust me, it won't go unnoticed. But you need to make this a priority. That way, she'll feel like there's always someone in her corner. Someone to fend for her. To take care of her. That it's you. That's not to suggest that she has carte blanche to treat you like her safety-slave. It's important to have boundaries and ground rules in a marriage, but we'll talk about that in our chapter on masculine containment. First, we are building a foundation of safety, which is necessary for boundaries to be effective and well received.

For the moment, however, just recognize that most of her emotional upset can be traced to one of these three things. So, the next time she is upset and it seems ridiculous or frustrating to you, ask: is it seen, special or supported? Let me give you some common examples I have heard countless times from my clients and decide for yourself which options to consider:

Let's start with this one. You're out for dinner with your wife. She gets cold and distant all-of-a-sudden and accuses you of checking out the waitress (which you were not, in fact, doing). Option one is to logically explain that you didn't, and spend the rest of the night trying desperately to convince her of this while she gets more and more hysterical and you get more and more angry. Option two is to recognize *she is not feeling special at that moment* and, because of your stellar insight, look her dead in the eyes and say "Why would I ever do that when I am sitting across from the most gorgeous woman in the entire restaurant?" This immediately gives her what she *actually needs* at that moment. Not what she says she wants, but what she *needs*, which is to feel special.

Next example. Your wife comes home from a stressful day at work and takes a shot at you about the disorganized shoes by the front door. Option one is to tell her all the other things you've done that day: picking up the kids, unclogging the sink, and cleaning up the kids' lunchboxes. Option two is to recognize she is feeling *unsupported* and say "Hey, I can tell you've had a hard day. The last thing I want is for you to see messy shoes the first thing when you walk in the room. Let me get those taken care of." If you handle it this way, she's very likely to calm down, regret her demeanor, and thank you in some way for the other things she knows you already did. Because it was *not actually about the shoes*, it was just about her feelings taking her over in that moment and her need to feel supported.

And finally, let's say your wife makes a comment about how you never listen to her in the same way that her friend Susie's husband, Tim, listens to Susie. Option one is to respond by telling her all the times you have listened to her, or make a comment about how Susie actually knows how to communicate, unlike your wife. This ensures the fight will escalate for the next hour or two (or year or two). The second option is to say "Hey, I really want you to feel like I understand you. Is there something specific I'm missing that you want to talk about?" You don't play into the passive aggression and cut right to the heart of the matter. This communicates that her ineffective communication is not the solution and that you can make her feel *seen*, which is what she really wants in that moment.

Now, in each of those examples, it can seem like *a lot* of effort. But remember, we are creating a foundation of safety here. This is not the pattern for the rest of your marriage. This is just to equip you with the tools to see what's *actually* going on so you can effectively address it as you see fit. Once you've established that you can do this, that you can make her feel safe in these three ways, she will trust you in a way you can't imagine. She will reconnect with you and respect you in ways that will blow your mind. At that point, you will finally be in a position to say "Hey, we are not going to speak that way to each other. I need you to take a breath and rephrase that in a respectful way." Understanding how to make her feel seen, special, and supported is a *huge piece* of what builds this foundation of respect so you can effectively set boundaries and expectations. But before we get to that in detail, we need to understand the process of rebuilding trust at a deeper level.

A Man's Work

As you've learned in this chapter, your wife won't explicitly say "I feel unsafe"—she'll just pull away. These two exercises are designed to help you read between the lines and build the trust she craves. Remember, when a woman feels seen, special, and supported, she softens. Don't wait for her to ask. Make safety your reflex. That's how kings lead with love.

1) Safety Mirror

Instructions: Write in your notebook about a moment this week when your wife seemed off. What happened? What did you do? Ask yourself: Was she feeling unseen, unspecial, or unsupported? Reflect on something you could've done differently (e.g., listened longer, complimented her). Try doing that next time. Do this daily to make her safety your instinctive priority.

Purpose: This develops awareness of her emotional needs and equips you with actionable responses.

2) Safety Signal Practice

Instructions: Make safety visible. Choose three small actions that make her feel loved—like a compliment, a chore, or asking about her day. Do one each day for a week. Watch how she responds—her tone, her eyes. Write it down. Don't think of this as a checklist: it's how you rebuild trust, one action and one day at a time.

Purpose: This encourages proactive behaviors to meet your wife's emotional needs, reinforcing her sense of safety.

Notes to Self

THE EIGHTH LAW: BUILD TRUST

At this point in the book, we've laid down most of the main foundations for a successful marriage. We began by establishing that you need to become a Sovereign Man, adding some moral, relational, and psychological muscle. This will help you to step up as the King of your own Kingdom: a man who can help to establish lasting peace, love, and happiness in his household. Next, we focused on the importance of being The Lighthouse to your wife's Storm—providing her with masculine stability amidst her feminine turmoil. To help you better understand your wife as a woman (and your role as a husband) we explored facts and feelings: how men see facts as facts, but women often see facts through their feelings. After that, we dove into the Love Switch and Mood Glasses: two concepts to help you navigate your wife's fluctuating emotions and outlook. This chapter discussed the importance of recognizing when her switch has turned off and her darkened glasses are on—and the loving things you can do to lift her spirits and transform her mood. Then we discussed the Fear Factor: how men often make their wives feel physically unsafe, as well as how you can help her feel emotionally safe—seen, special, and supported—so her soft feminine core can emerge.

Now that we're nearing the end of this book, we've only got a few foundational pieces left to put in place. Hence this chapter's focus on trust: both how to build it and how to maintain it. Once we've covered this, we can move on from the foundation. We can start to build the house—putting in some load-bearing walls, some windows and doors. I'll refer to this as providing masculine structure and helping you with it will be the final chapter's focus. But after that, it's your house to finish. But take courage from the fact that we're nearly there. You're nearly there.

Trust

Whether you're in a relationship's early stages or you've been together for a long time, trust is essential. It's indispensable, actually. To get off the ground, a relationship has to climb what I call the Ladder of Trust. Without it, there's no emotional security. No promise of consistency and reliability. Likewise, trust is what enables partners to give each other freedom and preserve their own individuality. I could go on, mentioning how greater trust results in deeper sexual intimacy and benefits other things like conflict resolution, but I hope you already know or at least sense all this. The bottom line, however, is simply this: trust is what enables two people to share one life together. That is what marriage is all about. It's a continual openness. It's endless sharing. Sometimes this is a beautiful thing, and sometimes it's brutal—but *it is* marriage. And the more trust there is between you, the sooner you'll move from merely surviving one another to thriving because of each other. Thriving because each of you feels fundamentally loved just as you are—not because of who you could be, should be, were or will be.

But trust takes time. It develops gradually. The ladder must be climbed one rung at a time. For men, though, the process is usually more straightforward. So long as the ladder looks reasonably steady, we climb it and we don't often come back down. You trust your wife and that's that. There may be small fluctuations and some minor things you might not trust her about, but at a fundamental level the trust is there. That's not to say your trust can't be eroded or destroyed, especially if you feel betrayed. But it would take a lot to bring you back down the ladder—let alone destroy it. But for a woman who's just beginning a relationship or is in the process of rebuilding one, the trust ladder works differently. For her, it needs to not only get built *one rung at a time*, but each new rung needs to be *tested* before she'll step on it. For that reason, she won't climb any higher than her current level of trust permits and she won't go any faster than her own sense of safety will allow.

Emotional Trust

Just as a woman won't feel physically safe without also feeling emotionally safe, so they won't trust someone without emotionally trusting them too—knowing a man's trustworthiness is not enough. She needs to *feel* it. But this takes time. And regardless of whether you're rebuilding trust or establishing it for the first time, there are a number of common obstacles that men face. As such, it's worth looking at these.

The first obstacle to gaining her trust is emotional distance. As in, you knock, but it seems like nobody's home. Whether it's talking about how her day went or asking about something bigger, like how her therapy is going, you can't seem to get anything from her. You find yourself frozen out, surviving on surface level scraps like what she had for lunch. Obviously, this is super frustrating. And if you've been in this situation before, you know all too well what this disconnection feels like—the lack of openness and transparency—and with it, the confusion. First, because when you bring up the problem, she either denies it or tries to downplay it. But secondly, it's confusing and hurtful because, after all, aren't you one of the good guys? I mean, you genuinely want to hear her thoughts and feelings. You're trustworthy. You keep secrets. You have integrity. You know this and she might even agree—and yet, she still doesn't open up.

A second obstacle is emotional reactivity. But I'm not talking about her reactivity—sensitive as she may be. I'm talking about you and the ways in which you've responded to what she's shared in the past. Because it doesn't take much for a man to signal to a woman (intentionally or not) that he's not safe to open up around. For example, if you've ever reacted to something she's said or done with anger, frustration, or, especially, judgment, she'll have taken notice. She'll have learned that opening up to you carries risks—and not just emotionally and relationally, but physically too, because remember, you're most likely a lot bigger and stronger than she is. And though not sharing deeper stuff with you may break her heart, she'd rather that than the fear of a broken bone (no matter how unfounded that fear is).

But here's the thing, even your subtle reactions—like pouting, withdrawing, or speaking with a sharp edge in your voice—sends a message. Namely, that she's not safe sharing certain things with you. This is true even if you just shut down and don't express any emotion at all—because it's frightening. It makes her think that you've become disconnected. That you don't love her. And if that's true, there's nobody to protect her from the proverbial saber-tooth tiger. And since she doesn't want you to feel that way about her, she stops sharing. She avoids anything that might push your buttons. Ironically, she'll often go too far in the opposite direction—making you feel even more disconnected—but as far as she's concerned, it's better to be safe than sorry.

The next obstacle is a lack of attention. This can be a question of both quantity and quality. She needs to have enough attention that she doesn't feel forgotten about, but that attention needs to be sufficiently high-grade that it doesn't feel like a token gesture. This may seem needy to some, but remember, men and women's needs are different. Just because she sees you every day—when you wake up together, have dinner, and watch a TV show together before bed—doesn't mean that she feels seen by you, let alone special and supported enough to truly open up.

This is especially true for couples who have fallen into established routines, co-managing daily life and dealing with kids, because days, weeks, and months can go by without deep conversation and meaningful connection. You might have noticed this, but I can guarantee that she's deeply *felt* it. So much so, the odd date night will no longer fix it. You may try a kind gesture, but that won't solve it either. That's because she needs to feel seen by you more than just once in a while. It needs to feel foundational. She needs to feel your full presence. Your real attention. I don't mean 24/7, of course, but there needs to be a consistency and regularity to it. A norm. Consider, for instance, how women connect with each other.

They do this by sharing information. When women first get into a friendship, they share very superficial details about their lives. But as they go deeper into the friendship, they start sharing more and more. At some point, when a woman recognizes someone as a really close friend, she'll start sharing secrets—about her marriage, about her friends. The deeper the sharing, the stronger the connection. Trust and sharing are *signals*—the more someone shares about what's truly going on in their world, the more it signals trust and connection to women. The same applies to you as her husband. If there isn't the time and space given for the mutual sharing of life's sometimes small, sometimes big issues and details, she'll (mis)interpret it as you not desiring a meaningful connection with her.

Another obstacle—and one that we've already covered—arises from men's tendency to jump straight to solutions. This usually happens when a woman brings up an issue—about work, a friend, or something personal—and instead of addressing her emotional reality, he tries to solve the situation for her. Of course, from the man's perspective, he's just trying to help. After all, people pay a lot of money for consultants to solve their problems and here he is, doing it pro bono—and not just for free, but often from a place of love. But here's the thing: most men aren't addressing the real problem. The real problem—the thing she actually wants fixing, so to speak—is her emotional concern. She wants to better understand how she feels about the situation. A man's job, therefore, is to listen. To ask questions. To be patient.

Being a good listener is important, because as communication experts will tell you, a person won't listen unless they feel like they've been listened to. She needs to be heard by you to hear from you. That's why your top priority is to make her feel understood. In all likelihood, she already knows the necessary solution, she just needs to take her own route to get there. A to B works great for men, but sometimes A to C to M to B works better for women. This can be frustrating, but if you try to go straight into problem-solving, she'll interpret it as you not caring. She'll think: *Oh, he doesn't actually care why this matters to me. He just wants to shut down the conversation. He doesn't want to understand—he just wants me to stop talking. And if he doesn't want to hear my problems, I won't share them anymore. I'll keep them to myself because he doesn't care.* Now, this is probably not the case at all. You no doubt care deeply (you're just bored by the level of detail she's sharing), but that's not how she'll emotionally interpret it—and that interpretation will shape how much she trusts you with her heart.

This ties in with another obstacle to gaining her trust, which is that she doesn't feel fully understood by you. This ties back to emotional reactivity and lack of attention. Sometimes this can be over big stuff, related to things like your finances or life-priorities. But it can just as easily be over the small things. For example, if she brings up something minor—she went to the grocery store and couldn't get the right beans to make the dinner she wanted to—and you brush past it with a quick, *Yeah, too bad*—she won't feel like you really get her. Trust begins with sharing details about her life—things as simple as what she did at the grocery store. So, let's say that instead of giving her a cursory answer when she told you about the beans, you stopped and took the time to engage with her. Perhaps you say something like "Oh, that must have been frustrating. I hate it when that happens." Trust me, I *know* how ridiculous that sounds. But for her, you've engaged. You've *connected*. It signals that it's safe to share things with you.

Now that you've built a little more trust, she feels safe enough to confide in you about a fight with Susie at the office. Again, you need to practice non-judgmental engagement. Show some interest and empathy. Because if you don't—if you say that it doesn't sound like a big deal or that Susie is just trying to get you to do your job and you need to respond to emails more quickly—you will be shutting her down. She'll think: *It's not safe to share this stuff. I'm not going any higher on the Trust Ladder.* But if you respond with something more neutral and empathetic—*Oh man, you know, I see Susie's point, but yeah, she could have communicated that in a much better way. She was really rude about it, and it seems like she undervalues the contributions you make at the office*—then she feels understood. She thinks, *Oh, okay, it's safe to share this interpersonal conflict with Susie.* That's not to say don't give her helpful advice. It's just to say that she needs to feel you emotionally resonating with her *before* she'll listen to such advice. When you create that emotional resonance effectively, she may feel comfortable opening up even more. Maybe she shares about a conflict within her family. Maybe she starts talking about something that isn't working in the relationship.

See how we've gone from beans all the way to deep problems in the relationship, one step at a time? And at the very highest level of trust—if she builds all the way there—she might share something deeply personal. Past trauma from childhood, long-held secrets, or something she's never told anyone before. But before she gets there, she needs to test whether it's safe at *each rung of the ladder*. At each level, she's looking for your reaction. Will you judge her and make her feel unsafe? Or will you be accepting, creating an environment where she can trust you with more? As you well know, this isn't the same way that men work—beans are just beans—but remember that in female-to-female relationships, the importance of a friendship can be determined very accurately by how much information each person is willing to share about their life. The more details they share, the closer the relationship becomes. In the same vein, even though you're in a male-to-female relationship, if you're not allowing her to share that kind of information with you—or if you're not interested in receiving it—that signals to her that you don't value the relationship very much. On the other hand, if she feels safe enough to share all kinds of information with you and you're willing to receive it—at least up to a certain point (because men don't have an infinite capacity to hear about beans)—that tells her you really value the relationship. It shows her that she's in your inner circle.

The last obstacle is a lack of follow-through. If she observes, over time, that you don't follow through on your commitments—whether in your personal habits, your career, or even basic self-care—she will start to see you as untrustworthy. You say one thing, but do another. Now, you might be great about doing all the big-ticket items. You've never cheated on her, you've provided for her, etc., etc., but this is about the small, everyday moments. This may seem insignificant to you—who cares if you didn't change the car's oil when you said you would, or that you haven't made it to gym even though you've been saying you would for six weeks—but I promise you, the cumulative impact of these let-downs is significant to her. In her eyes, you're not being a man of your word. She thinks *this is not a man who does what he says he's going to do.* And that, gentlemen, is a big deal. She will assume this is true in your relationship just as it is in your personal habits.

From her perspective, if she believes that you won't follow-through on the little things, there's no reason to entrust you with the big things. Indeed, she might not even think that you take her seriously. Because let's be honest, we don't blow off the really important things in life—not unless we want to be fired, imprisoned, abandoned or whatever else might befall those who don't keep their word or honor their obligations. That's why, if she shares something important—if she tells you, *Hey, this hurts me when you do this,* and you promise to change but keep doing it, that will be *far worse* than if you had never made the promise at all. Because at that point, it's not just about the action—it's about *whether she matters to you at all.* You may know that she does, but she doesn't feel like she does—and that cuts deep.

To-Do List

So, what can you do to build trust? You can begin by focusing on non-judgmental engagement. If she opens up about something—again with the beans—don't shut her down by being apathetic, glib, or distracted. Engage with her. Relate to her. Make her feel like she's a part of your inner-circle by allowing yourself to be a part of hers. This will really help to establish some trust: as in, she'll believe that it's okay to talk to you about stuff. And because she doesn't feel judged about bringing up the little things, she'll be more willing to entrust you with the more important stuff.

The change won't be immediate and it has to develop over time, but it can be helped along by doing simple and specific things. For instance, one of the most powerful ways to build trust is through personal discipline. When she sees you consistently following through—going to the gym, putting in effort at work, staying late when necessary, keeping commitments with the kids—her trust in you deepens. The specifics don't really matter. What matters is consistent, relatable actions. If you put in the work, she'll notice the shift. She may reward you with sharing a detail about her day or talking about a struggle at work. In time, as you continue to build trust, she'll open up about deeper things. So long as you respond in a way that reassures her—making her feel safe, seen, and special—her trust in you will keep growing.

The most important thing is to start small. Remember, the ladder of trust can only get built one rung at a time. Don't overpromise. Immediately becoming the perfect husband isn't a realistic goal. That's like a white-belt trying to jump straight to black belt. She'll sense it's not real. Even if your efforts last a week or two, she'll likely think: *This won't last.* Focus instead on being reliable in the small things and the bigger things will either come in time or take care of themselves. Just keep showing up. Keep following through. Keep proving, through your actions, that you are steady and trustworthy. Over time, the ladder will get both stronger and higher. When she senses that the next rung is strong enough to step on, she'll climb it—because deep down, every woman wants to be able to trust her man.

Another method for building trust is improving your everyday communication. For example, think about something as simple as a text exchange. Suppose she messages you about a change in plans. If the change affects your schedule, you might feel frustrated. But instead of reacting emotionally—getting upset or irritated—respond with understanding. This doesn't mean you have to agree with the change or always accommodate her requests. You can still assert your boundaries while showing empathy. But instead of replying negatively—texting that this isn't fair, that it's screwing you over, that you've already talked about this—write back with a demonstration of understanding and empathy. You might text, "I understand where you're coming from, and I know this is important to you." Even if you ultimately say no, the way you communicate makes all the difference. She will start to notice: *Oh, his responses feel different. He's seeing me.* That alone deepens trust.

This applies whether you're in a new relationship, trying to reconnect in a strained one, or even separated. It's not just the big conversations that matter—it's the small, daily interactions. Passing each other in the hall, discussing schedules, answering quick questions—it's how you handle these moments that determines whether trust grows or erodes. Are you thoughtful, supportive, and understanding, or are you distracted, judgmental, or uncooperative? Know that a woman will pick up on subtleties like body language and tone of voice that will pass most men by. We tend to communicate more directly, so a small change in how we text or speak might seem insignificant to us. But to her, those shifts carry weight. If she notices, *Oh, he actually wants to understand why I need to change the plans. He actually cares why I feel this way,* she will register that difference—even over text.

If you have three, four, or five conversations like that in a row, she will take stock of it. And when she starts feeling heard and understood, she will feel *more attracted to you.* Then you can begin to build on that. It starts small—better conversations, better responses. Then maybe a date. Then sitting together on the couch, reconnecting in a way you haven't in a long time. Then deeper emotional intimacy. Then physical intimacy. You can get there in a matter of weeks. It can go from *She never tells me anything* to *She's opening up about things she's never told anyone, even after 20 years of marriage.* But it happens step by step, one rung of the ladder at a time.

Trust, But Verify

By now, this might be sounding easy enough. Take time, build trust, reap the reward. But I'm afraid it's not as simple as that. There's a snag. As your wife comes to trust you more and as your intimacy grows, there will come a time when she feels the need to stress-test the ladder. In essence, she realizes she has moved from the first rung on the trust ladder to the second. Then, in hindsight, she notices, *Oh, shoot, I'm at a new level of safety and connection with this guy.* And that realization can trigger fear. *Is this really safe? What if it's all been fake? What if he's been lying, pretending the whole time?* A very effective way to find out if you're for real or just faking it is to *pick a fight with you* and really piss you off. She doesn't initiate The Test consciously, but instinctively. Deep down, on a subconscious level, she knows that if you crack under the pressure and the mask drops, you're not for real. That you can't actually be trusted. But if she can't break you—if you remain calm, steady, and present—then she realizes, *Oh, it was actually real. He is absolutely the one.*

It's a harsh test, but it's incredibly effective. As the old Russian proverb goes, *trust, but verify.* There are probably many reasons why many women unconsciously resort to this, but it likely comes from an ancient instinct. As we've discussed, historically, women chose male partners not just for companionship but for protection. They needed someone capable of violence to keep them and their children safe. But how do you know if a man's capacity for violence is truly safe? How do you ensure that when you have a child with him and are tied to him for the next 15 years, he won't turn that violence on you or the child? You could analyze his track record, talk to his friends, and make a logical assessment. Or, you could do something far more *effective*—you could push all his buttons, drive him to the edge of his capacity, and then do your best to push him over. If he stands tall, he's safe; he's the one. But if he loses control—he's a danger. He's not safe. He's not the one.

Perhaps you've been through this before. If you haven't you can expect it to occur when the attraction and trust between you is returning. It often happens once she's become more engaged and affectionate. It may come after you've had a great evening together—a meaningful date, a deep conversation, or even just a warm, connected chat. It'll likely come when you're feeling *really good* in the relationship. Often after a major reconnection or a "win" of some kind. Then, suddenly, the next day, she seemingly *loses it* over something tiny. It's like you're back to square one, but crazier. The temptation here is to lean into your instinctive reaction—that yesterday was a smoke screen or a mirage. That it was just a temporary calming of an otherwise screwed up and crazy storm. Feeling this, it's all too easy to think that your wife is actually insane or mentally ill—like she's a narcissist or bipolar. After all, if a guy acted this way—if one day everything was wonderful and the next, he was raging over nothing—it would make no sense to us. But remember, your wife is not a guy.

This can be one of the most frustrating moments in a relationship. It doesn't help that it often occurs just as you're hitting your stride. When you've been making changes, following through, and reaping the reward of greater closeness. Plus, the fact that she picks a fight over something so trivial, comes as one hell of a curveball. There's no pretending that when this happens it isn't painful, exasperating and often deeply demoralizing—but keep your chin up, because it actually represents a real victory. Again, it's not a loss. *The Test always feels like a loss, but if you handle it correctly it is always a win.* Your wife is testing you because she *wants* you, not because she doesn't.

Of course, it's possible that she picks a fight with you at other points, for other reasons. For example, she could be feeling ignored and if she's not getting the attention she craves, even negative attention might feel better than nothing. A fight at least proves you're emotionally engaged. It's not a healthy dynamic, but it's common. Likewise, she might be feeling unloved and hopes that a strong emotional reaction from you—even if it's anger or frustration—will feel like proof that you still care. So too, if she's uncertain about the relationship or feeling disconnected, provoking an argument might be her way of forcing some engagement. Or she may just need to vent. But the point I'm trying to make is that these things are different from The Test. Though you may need to respond to these things in similar ways—making sure that she feels safe, seen, special, and supported—The Test is different. It comes when things are going well. Really well. And though you may not like the way she is testing you, the fact that she's testing you is a good thing. It represents a win! Remember that she's not doing this consciously, but instinctively—it's an evolutionary thing. So take courage because it's a very good sign, and so long as you pass, it'll take you to even better wins in the future.

How She Tests You

As we've established, the primary way she tests you is by picking a fight—seemingly out of nowhere. She does this to jolt you into a bad mood or a dark place. She then manufactures stress, tension, and emotional chaos to see if your behavior is genuine or just a temporary front. Remember, except in rare cases, this is not intentional manipulation. It is an unconscious test of her safety, "is it safe to go to the next level of trust and intimacy with this man?" A key sign of a test fight is that it follows noticeable improvement in your relationship. If things have been getting better—more intimacy, more affection, more connection—then a sudden fight that comes out of nowhere is likely a test. It'll feel like a complete 180. One moment, everything is great; the next, it seems like all that progress has vanished. If you find yourself thinking, *What the hell just happened?* That's when you know.

Another sign is that what she's upset about is trivial, irrational, or contradictory. She asks for oranges, then gets mad you didn't bring apples. She tells you to do something a certain way, you follow it exactly, and she's still upset. It doesn't make sense, and that's the trap. The irrationality *is the point.* She's not upset about the oranges—she's creating a situation to see how you handle it. Unfortunately, no matter what the scenario or pretext is, anything you say will just make it worse. In a normal argument, you can de-escalate by acknowledging her emotions, helping her get clarity, and being supportive. But in a test fight, every attempt to calm her down or reason with her will escalate things. If you're being reasonable, she gets angrier. If you reassure her, she acts as if you're dismissing her. Nothing will be the right response. As the fight escalates, she'll press your buttons. She'll bring up past mistakes, throw your insecurities in your face, and say things designed to get under your skin. You'll feel like you're talking to a completely different person, an insane person. If it continues, she might cross the line into insults and personal attacks, looking for any moment where you lose your cool and prove this 'new you' isn't real. In a situation like this, the only thing you can do—the only way to pass—is to recognize it for what it is and not engage. Stay calm, unshaken, and refuse to be pulled into the chaos. Otherwise, if you take the bait, react emotionally, or lose control, you automatically fail.

I know this isn't easy. That it's brutally hard. It will push you to the edge of what you can handle emotionally, and you'll absolutely be close to losing your cool. In fact, that's really the point of it. So expect a moment to rise where you think, *Screw this. I don't deserve this. I'm done.* But it's crucial that you do not react. Even if she starts attacking you with your past failures or weaknesses, even if she makes you feel like less of a man or that you begin to question yourself and your commitment to her—hold on. The whiplash that you're feeling is your cue. That's the moment to remind yourself, *This is a test.* Hold onto the fact that she's on the verge of deeper connection—and she wants to go there. She wouldn't test you if she didn't want to believe in the relationship, if she didn't want to trust what's happening between you. She just needs proof that it's safe. Deep in her mind, her subconscious thoughts are saying, *If you can handle this—this chaos I'm throwing at you—then maybe you really are as safe as I've been feeling. Maybe I can keep opening myself up to you emotionally, spiritually, sexually.* Granted, in the middle of a test you may not feel like it's worth it, but it will be. Indeed, it will be more than worth it.

Passing The Test

The single most important thing to do… is the thing that you mustn't do. *Do not storm back.* Let me say it again, DO NOT STORM BACK. If you do, you'll confirm her worst fear—that your patience, kindness, and stability weren't real, that they were just a temporary act. The moment you lose your cool, she thinks, *Oh, I see. He was pretending.* She'll believe that she was right not to trust you and once she believes that, she pulls away—hard. As such, when she's in full meltdown mode—saying things that make no sense, contradicting herself, escalating with every response—the worst thing you can do is argue, try to prove her wrong, or justify yourself. Even if she is wrong, it doesn't matter. Instead of explanations or corrections, use steady, validating responses. Something like, "That must be hard for you. I'm sorry I hurt you. I didn't mean to make you feel that way." If she throws accusations—*You did this! You never do that!*—keep things simple, saying, "That's not how I wanted you to feel. That must have been awful for you." Of course, don't say it like a robot or an actor practicing his lines, mix your responses up a little, but words like these will go a long way.

Just remember that it's not about whether her complaints are *true*. It's about what she needs to *feel* at that moment. David Deida puts it perfectly in *The Way of the Superior Man*, "Her complaints are content-free." This doesn't mean her feelings aren't real, but the thing she's pointing to—the laundry, the oranges—isn't the real issue. If you take the factbait and argue about laundry, you have already lost. Keep in mind that she doesn't see that she's being unreasonable. Likewise, no amount of logic will make her stop and say, *Oh wow, you're right. Thanks for clearing that up.* That will *never happen*. The only thing to do is be present, steady, and supportive. Once she calms down and reconnects with you emotionally, *then* you can have a real conversation. But in the moment, engaging will only make things spiral further.

As frustrating as it sounds, she will… tire herself out. She'll push and push, vent and storm, until her energy starts to dip, her outbursts lose intensity, and she slows down. That's your signal the test is winding down—not because you fixed anything, but because she needed to feel her way through it. The only problem is that she won't tire out as quickly as you'd like. It will last longer than feels bearable. It will push you past your known-limits. And that's intentional. From her perspective, it's supposed to. Because if you stay calm, patient, and grounded, she begins to believe in you in a way she didn't before. Just keep in mind that she's not trying to consciously manipulate you. She's not playing mind games, scheming, or trying to make your life miserable. Women don't process emotions the way men do—they feel their way through the world. That's what makes them intuitive lovers and incredible mothers. When her Love Switch is on, she sees what you need before you recognize it yourself. But that same emotional intuition also means she can be volatile in ways that don't make sense to you. If you apply a male lens to this—if you think, *If my buddy did this, he'd be insane*—you're missing the point. She's not wired like you. If you judge her emotions through a strictly logical framework, you'll end up resenting her, believing women are irrational and impossible. That's how so many men fall into bitterness, isolation, and resentment. Women aren't awful. They're just different. And this is part of that difference.

Once you've passed the test, your wife now knows that if you're pushed to the edge, you won't collapse. You won't lash out. You won't revert to old habits. Your strength and power as a man is *deep*. Your presence is *bigger* than her emotions. And this is when something shifts inside of her. The fight that seemed like it was going to destroy everything actually deepens your connection, strengthens intimacy, and builds unshakable trust. In no time she'll climb higher up the ladder than she's ever gone before—or at least higher than she's been for a long, long time. And that's all because you proved—through your presence, steadiness, and unwavering love—that you are safe. That you can handle all of her, even the wild, chaotic, emotional parts. Now you're ready to enjoy what comes next.

Delayed Gratitude

Unfortunately, you can't expect an immediate reward. She won't suddenly smile, apologize, and jump into your arms. More likely, she'll say, *You just don't get it. You're not the man I need.* She might storm out, hang up, or leave the house. But that's fine. It's not ideal, but it's not a problem. As long as she's walking away angry *because you stayed calm*, YOU WON. It doesn't matter that she's still upset. She needs to cool-off. To settle down. In the meantime, take some pride in the fact that you didn't let yourself get pulled into the chaos. You did exactly what you needed to do. You were *bigger*. If, however, she's storming off because you lost your cool, because you shouted, snapped, or got defensive, then you didn't pass. She may give you another shot in the months to come, but it is going to take longer and be harder than before. If this is the case, it might be time to acknowledge that you need more help. If so, think about getting in contact with me in order to get more personalized support using the contact info at the end of this book.

But let's assume you didn't fail. You won! So, where is your reward? It's coming, but it won't be instantaneous. She won't instantly recognize what just happened or thank you. This is where *delayed gratitude* comes in. If you're new to this, expect it to take hours or even days, before she comes back. That said, it's rare for it to take more than 48-72 hours. Usually it's just a few hours. But when she does come back, she really comes back—radically softer. She'll likely return to you, a few hours later, maybe a day or two, as a far softer, more nurturing, and more appreciative wife than you have *ever* had. There's a good chance that your sex life will be at a new, more exciting place as well. She now knows you can handle *all* of her—so she wants to *give you all of her*, emotionally, mentally, spiritually, and physically. I cannot tell you the number of clients I have who quickly learned to be *excited* for the Tests–because new and amazing sex always followed.

Other signs will show up too. You might catch her looking at you differently—that soft, admiring gaze some guys call Bambi eyes. She might initiate intimacy, treat you with more respect, or even say, *I'm sorry about that. You handled it really well*. But don't expect words right away. More often, she'll show her gratitude through her actions. And here's the thing—you won't need to ask if you passed. You'll know, trust me. The energy between you will be transformed. She will feel different. Now she can fully open up to you. And when she believes that? Everything changes.

To switch out metaphors from ladders to video games, you've just succeeded against the boss that comes at the end of a level. You're Mario, The Test was Bowser. Well done, now you get to level-up. It might sound silly, but it's exactly how trust works in a relationship. Relationships move through levels—each requiring deeper emotional safety, intimacy, and trust. Every time you get to the end of a new level, a test arrives to confirm whether the connection is real. If you pass, the bond deepens. The game gets better. The rewards become greater. The downside, however, is that after passing a test, even though you'll experience a period of deeper connection—maybe for days, weeks, even months—another test will eventually come. But even though the levels and the bosses change, and the difficulty of each level increases, your strategy remains the same. Don't enter the storm. Remain calm. Wait it out. Love her through it. After you've passed this next test and four or five more, there comes an Apex Storm. You reach the end of the final level and face Bowser in his final form. It is a Test for the ages. A storm like you've never seen. It'll likely be a result of something *tiny*: a misplaced sock, a comment you made on the phone, the take-out dish you bring home to her… it will be END OF THE WORLD. But, if you remain The Lighthouse… something shifts after this Test. You've hit a turning point.

So, if things are going *really well* for a long enough time, expect the Apex Storm. Expect that you will *feel* like things are "definitely over," as many clients have texted me during their wives' Apex Storms. But, if it's an *insane* fight for some *insane* reason and the level of intensity is also… *insane*… Congratulations. The worst part of healing a damaged relationship is almost over. You have sunny skies ahead. Remind yourself of this. Hear my voice in your head, "This is it!! The Apex Storm! You're almost there!"

When this happens, and you pass, the tests stop being as frequent or severe—because she now trusts you to such an extent that she no longer feels the need to challenge it. Though the tests won't disappear entirely, they become substantially less dramatic, less common, and far easier to handle. Not to mention you've effectively made yourself into Super Mario—so there's that. I want to highlight this for you: once you get past the Apex Storm the tests become *less and less frequent* and *less and less intense* over time.

Instead of feeling like the world is collapsing every few weeks, the tests shrink into small emotional check-ins. There's no more mind-warping, emotionally brutal fights—just brief, contained moments that barely disrupt the relationship. For example, in my relationship with Whitney, I still face tests, but they're nothing like before. The last one we had on a date night ended before we finished our appetizers—no big fight, no lingering tension, just a quick moment that passed followed by immediate increased connection. That's what happens when deep trust is built. The tests don't vanish, but they shrink into minor bumps instead of massive explosions. And the benefits—the softness, the connection, the great sex, the Bambi eyes… they become the new normal in your day-to-day married life.

The amazing thing is that as unbearable as these tests feel at first, when you come out on the other side, you realize two things. Firstly, *her Storms aren't actually that bad.* They aren't the existential threats you once thought they were—and you no longer have to feel threatened by them. It becomes easy to stay calm. Your depth of presence as a man has increased, your confidence and unshakability are more solid. When this happens, you might find yourself *so unfazed* that you struggle not to chuckle at her when she is storming. Second, you realize: *I now actually have the woman I always wanted.* To your genuine delight, you'll find that she wants to take care of you. She wants to be close. She does things for you, not out of obligation, but because she desires it. Desires you. She brags about you. She tells you how much she admires you and appreciates your sacrifices. And once you've been through this cycle enough times, the tests stop feeling like something to fear. Instead, you recognize them for what they are: proof that deeper connection and affection is right around the corner—and that's always a good thing.

A Man's Work

Trust isn't built by words—it's earned by your actions over time. These two exercises help you spot where you've gained ground and where you've slipped. Remember that when she sees you as steady, her heart follows. Don't aim for perfection—aim for presence. Track it. Improve it. Trust is a ladder—it gets built (and climbed) one rung at a time.

1) Trust-Building

Instructions: Trust grows in actionable moments. Each day for a week, look back on the day and write about a moment when you could've built trust but didn't. Perhaps this was about keeping a promise or simply listening to her. Reflect on what you did and didn't do. How did she respond to that? What could you do better tomorrow? Keep a log and celebrate your wins.

Purpose: This helps you track trust-building efforts and identifies growth areas.

2) Commitment Audit

Instructions: Kings keep their word. List five promises you've made—like date nights or finances. Rate how well you've kept each (1–10). For each, write one improvement. Choose one and act on it. Ask her, "Did that feel good to you?" Review monthly. Reliability isn't flashy—but it's everything.

Purpose: This reinforces reliability, a cornerstone of trust.

Notes to Self

THE NINTH LAW: ESTABLISH BOUNDARIES

Water is a powerful, elemental force. It has the capacity to support life as well as destroy it. For thousands of years, humans have built their homes along riverbanks, knowing that despite their dangers, these waterways are special—that without them, human development on a large scale would be practically impossible. Just think about it: without the Thames, we wouldn't have London. No Seine, no Paris; no Hudson, no New York. That's not just because these rivers are essential for everything from freshwater to navigation and trade; it's also because rivers have their own beautiful, almost mystical allure.

But as everybody knows, water can also be dangerous. Rivers can break their banks. They have the power to drown and destroy. In 1931, for instance, the Yangtze, Huai, and Yellow Rivers overflowed, submerging huge swaths of China. The floods killed as many as four million people. But you don't have to go as far away as the Orient to see a river's destructive potential. Here in the United States, the Great Mississippi Flood of 1993 caused over $15 billion worth of damage, wreaking havoc across nine different states. In both cases, prolonged and torrential downpours were partly to blame—but here's the thing about floods: they're often our fault too.

Floods happen. Everyone knows that, but not everyone builds good dikes. Not everyone invests in efficient levees or maintains strong embankments. Some do—just look at Holland. Almost a quarter of the country is below sea level, but you don't see the Dutch drowning. But that's because they've future-proofed their present. They've built for tomorrow's flood, today. In essence, they've done the hard work. They've spent the money and done the right things. But sadly, not everyone does that. Sure, they've got their excuses. Investing in flood protection isn't cheap. The politics aren't easy. The planning takes forever. But when the waters suddenly rise and the flood now threatens, ask yourself where you'd rather be: Holland or somewhere that isn't all that prepared. I know where I'd rather be and I'm sure you do too.

Of course, I'm not suggesting that we all move to Holland. That's not the point. Instead, I brought up rivers because whether you realize it or not, you're married to one. That's because, metaphorically speaking, a woman's feminine energy is a lot like a river. It, too, flows. It connects, supports, and nourishes. Whereas your masculine energy is structured, logical, action-oriented, and goal-focused, her feminine energy is more open, receptive, flowing, and expressive. Neither is better and both work best when paired together—not least because like a river, her feminine energy requires direction and banks, boundaries and structures, otherwise, its flow can turn into a flood—becoming chaotic, overwhelming, and unstable. This is why many women who have spent years being single or who have never experienced a healthy masculine presence may seem emotionally scattered, constantly overwhelmed, or struggling to find stability. Lacking banks, they flow in every direction searching for some kind of structure to flow within. They're searching for something dependable enough to hold them—so they feel safe enough to let go, unwind, relax, and truly be themselves. Your role as a husband is to help with that, by providing Masculine Structure, which includes setting healthy boundaries.

It's important to stress that Masculine Structure is not about controlling women. Masculinity doesn't mean "the patriarchy". A man's leadership shouldn't require a woman's subservience. Instead, Masculine Structure is about holding and channeling feminine energy in ways that lead to greater emotional, physical, and psychological well-being. To go back to our waterway's metaphor, it's about strengthening a river's banks and natural (as well as man-made) flood defenses, which is not the same thing as controlling or damming the river. Quite the opposite, in fact. A river's identity and purpose are found as it flows to the sea—and the banks and flood defenses help the river to do just that. Indeed, the structure and support they provide serve the river's own interests, because flooding doesn't help a river's waters reach the sea (never mind the destruction that's caused by the flooding). And in much the same way, the purpose of Masculine Structure is not to stifle or control a woman's feminine energy. It's to help it flow with strength, grace, and purpose, rather than spilling chaotically across the land—or in this case, your lives and your relationship.

But to do this, you'll have to step up. To be more like the Dutch. Because in most healthy relationships—and despite the fact that men and women both have masculine and feminine characteristics—it's the masculine partner who leads in this area, providing the right structure for the feminine partner's energy to flow. This dynamic—when healthy—creates deep trust, attraction, and stability. It turns homes into happier, safer places. But like the people living on actual floodplains, the choice is yours. You can build Masculine Structure into your marriage or not, but both you and your wife will benefit if you do. The opposite is true if you don't.

Masculine Structure

So, what exactly do I mean when I talk about Masculine Structure? In essence, it's the creation and maintenance of healthy boundaries, embracing accountability, taking on responsibility, and providing your partner with a steady personal presence—physically, emotionally, and mentally. It's about creating an environment where she can trust, relax, and thrive because she knows the man she is with is steady, reliable, and present. In essence, it's leadership. In some ways, it's an extension of the leadership you've already taken in your own life—transforming yourself from slave to sovereign—but now that leadership is being turned outward. But it's not the kind of leadership that crowns you as the CEO or captain of your marriage, let alone dictator. Instead, it's leadership of another kind. A more thoughtful, serving, and loving leadership. Yes, it resembles a wise, Sovereign King, but it's a king who's more interested in serving than being served. A King who enables his kingdom to thrive—not by marginalizing or undermining its queen, but by strengthening the queen herself. It's concerned with her rule too.

As mentioned, a lack of structure helps no one. In its absence, women often feel more alone, overwhelmed, and unsafe. Over time, this erodes their emotional, mental, and physical reserves, leaving them more anxious, resentful, and disconnected. When that happens, their capacity to "pour into you"—to bring warmth, positivity, and energy into the relationship—diminishes. A woman's cup needs to feel sufficiently full if she's going to pour into you. In a sense, she needs the right input *from you* in order to give the right output *to you*. If she's feeling drained, neglected, or negative, you're going to experience a lot of negativity from her. That's just how it works. You might be different—you might stand tall even when you feel small, like a wounded soldier still fighting on—but that's testosterone at play, not estrogen. Your wife needs to feel *nurtured* to be *nurturing*, *supported* to be *supportive, and stable* in order to offer *stability*. But as you well know, it's not just the woman who suffers when there's a lack of structure. Men do too.

When a woman floods, the man will often feel bewildered, disrespected, and unappreciated. It may cause him to question his worth and perhaps even his entire identity. In short, a flood isn't pretty. But on the flip side, when a man fully embodies Masculine Structure, not only does his partner become softer, warmer, and more nourishing, he will also feel more desired, respected, and proud. He will experience a new kind of marital harmony, because the relationship enjoys balance—a kind of polarity, with both a north and south pole creating magnetism and dynamic play. This in turn gives his marriage a new lease of life and sets them up to enjoy a lifetime of marital success. And yet, despite this, a lot of men shy away from owning this role. This is to no one's benefit.

One reason is that men struggle to understand or implement Masculine Structure, often because they've had few such role models. The dominant portrayals of men in media—such as Homer Simpson or other clueless, passive husbands—do not show men providing stability, leadership, or protection. And it doesn't help that a lot of guys have grown up with either absent or abusive fathers, leaving them without a positive model to grow into and build on. As a result, they enter adulthood without a clear sense of how to lead with strength and stability. But those aren't the only reasons. Modern culture also discourages masculine leadership. Post-feminist narratives reject the idea of Masculine Structure, framing it as outdated or oppressive. The upshot is that a huge number of men suppress their natural leadership instincts, fearing they'll be labelled as sexist or misogynistic. Then, lacking both a sense of purpose and potential, many of these guys turn in on themselves and in the process, turn their backs on others. But it doesn't have to be this way. Masculinity can indeed turn toxic, just as femininity can—but properly understood and wisely embodied—it can help to heal a marriage. Indeed, it can help to heal an entire land. Because there's a world of difference between leadership and tyranny—and that difference starts with you and the positive change you can create in your own marriage.

Unfortunately, without positive examples, the majority of men don't get masculinity right. On the one hand are the 'nice guys'. These men are passive, approval-seeking, and lacking boundaries. They are overly accommodating and avoid conflict as a matter of principle—or survival. The nice guy believes that by being agreeable and compliant, he will win approval. But in actual fact, he creates an environment of uncertainty and frustration that handicaps himself and his partner—requiring her to develop a hard outer shell in the absence of his protection. On the other hand, is the 'tyrant', or 'asshole'. These men are overly rigid, controlling, and dismissive. They see relationships as power struggles and impose rules to satisfy their selfish desires not to serve those they care for. Rather than creating structures, the asshole creates an oppressive, suffocating environment. They act from fear rather than love.

A healthy, positive masculinity exists between and above these two extremes—strong, but loving; firm, but understanding. It is not about forcing or dominating, nor is it about bending over backwards to please. It is about presence, responsibility, and leadership that invites a woman's trust, rather than demands her obedience. It creates structures in which others can thrive. Let me give you a few examples of what I mean.

Masculine Structure should provide everyone with a sense of certainty. For that to happen, you need to be decisive in your decision-making and take full ownership of your choices. This isn't about enforcing a *my way or the highway* approach or making unilateral decisions for both of you. But it does require direction and follow-through. If you and your wife agree to eat healthier, don't just nod along—take ownership. Plan meals, do the grocery shopping, or start cooking more nutritious meals yourself. If her enthusiasm wanes, encourage her. You don't need to become the kitchen commandant—you can always agree to adjust things later—but she should know she's got backup. That the commitment to healthier eating isn't all on her shoulders. But deep down, the healthy eating isn't really about the healthy eating, just as the dishes aren't really about the dishes. The certainty you provide in the small things comes from a deeper certainty about yourself. That means knowing and acting on—rather than ignoring—your values and direction in life. If you don't have clarity about this, get it. Put in the work. Because you can't be the man you should be if you have no idea who that man is.

Another key aspect of Masculine Structure is vision and direction. This means having a clear path to follow—*leading*, not drifting. Take retirement as an example. You and your wife have agreed that saving for it is a priority. So, every month, you make sure the right amount is set aside, even if that means making sacrifices. When those sacrifices start to hurt, you lead the charge—not by complaining or capitulating, but by finding creative solutions or simply standing firm. You remain courageous but calm, empathetic but steadfast. It won't always be easy. If your wife wants something you can't afford—whether it's a longer holiday or a bigger house—you're strong enough to hold fast. But you also show understanding and compassion toward her material and emotional needs. Of course, there will be times when a strategic compromise is necessary. But when that happens, it comes from a place of strength and collective purpose—not from shortsightedness, directionlessness, or being badgered into poor decisions. Remember, she will not trust your guidance if you do not trust yourself—and stick to what you know is right.

The other elements of Masculine Structure will already be familiar to you, because we've talked about the importance of providing emotional stability. That's being The Lighthouse. It's also not overreacting when her Love Switch flicks off and her darkened Mood Glasses are on. It's not taking the factbait or jumping into the Storm with her. It's making sure she feels safe, seen, special, and supported. So, too, we've covered how, through a mixture of service and leadership, you can take a leading role in building trust between you: one rung at a time. But one of the most important aspects of Masculine Structure is setting boundaries and firmly (but fairly) upholding them—and that's what we're going to cover next in much greater detail.

Personal Boundaries

Setting boundaries in a relationship is essential, especially when certain issues persist. When this happens, you need to be able to say "This needs to happen," or "This needs to stop happening." Not that every boundary needs to be framed exactly like this. There are, in fact, two types of boundaries. The first kind are explicit. These are the lines you've drawn in the sand. They're direct and verbal. For example, you might tell your wife that "I need you to stop bringing up your ex in arguments," "I will not engage in name-calling," or "I expect honesty about finances." These are helpful for instigating specific and often new behavioral expectations.

The second kind are natural, implicit boundaries. These are usually unspoken and are developed over time. They are earned, not implemented—naturally emerging from the maintenance of your own high personal standards. For instance, a de facto boundary might emerge around finances: that you always check with each other first before expensive purchases; or surrounding socializing:

that you don't invite friends to stay the weekend without ensuring that it's okay. Whatever your particular rule is, natural boundaries get respected because *she respects you*. Because she wants to avoid behaviors that would hurt you. And that's why it's important to progress from explicit boundaries to natural ones in the long term—because they're both a sign and a product of trust. It's her intuitively desiring to honor your standards, without you even needing to verbalize them, because she trusts and respects you: the man behind them. The man who embodies them.

Let's say that you set the boundary at name-calling. Her first instinct will be to test that boundary—is it genuine or just a mirage? To that end, she may call you more names. Then even worse names, upping the emotional ante. But again, this is not *only* defiance. She's very simply finding out if this boundary is real. She's testing for cracks in the wall. How you respond in that moment determines whether the boundary is successful. If you react with anger, shouting, or slamming doors, you undermine the very safety you are trying to create. You prove that you are not a Wise King capable of upholding a healthy order in your kingdom—you are the pretty Tyrant King. So, instead, the correct approach is to maintain emotional calm and simply state, "I'm not willing to be spoken to that way, so I'm going to step away from this conversation. We can come back to it when we're both in a better place to talk." At this point, don't expect her to fold. At least, not yet. She may follow you, demand that you continue the conversation, or escalate her frustration. But this is where follow-through is crucial. If you re-engage and start arguing again, she will learn that your boundary *is not real*. If, however, you remain calm and repeat, "I told you I'm not having this conversation right now. I'll be happy to talk later, but I'm not engaging this way." Note that your focus is on the boundary: your mention of her behavior is indirect. This keeps things objective and less emotionally charged for you. At some point, she'll see that you're not budging and then, over time, she'll come to respect the boundary. Just keep in mind that the more consistently you enforce the boundary, *the more secure she will feel in the relationship.*

This might sound patronizing, but a woman's initial response to boundary-setting can be very similar to how children respond. When you set a firm rule—"This is a line you don't cross with Daddy"—they might initially push back in an effort to discover if the boundary is real, but over time, they settle into that structure because they recognize that *the same walls that keep them inside also keep threats out*. Since your children are young, you don't expect them to 100% respect the boundary at first—so you practice firm but caring patience, knowing that in the long run you've got this. You keep in mind that a household with clear rules and expectations is a safe household. A happier one, too, and most restful for the sensitive nervous systems of young children. So take courage from this, because the same principle applies to your marriage. If she perceives you as a man without boundaries or follow through, she won't trust you to keep her safe in a broader sense. But if you set and maintain healthy, mature, and loving boundaries, she will lean on you more and trust your leadership. She will realize the structure around the relationship is solid, secure, and fair. So, maybe for the first time ever, she can finally *relax* inside of those walls and *let her own guard down*. And, when this happens, you will not need to enforce these boundaries constantly. She will actually *appreciate* them, content in the rest that your structure allows her. If this sounds impossible for your wife, trust that I have likely seen it happen in worse circumstances. Over and over and over.

The key is first and foremost to maintain your stance with calm consistency. If you lose your temper, yell back, or slam the door, you undermine the boundary and make future enforcement even harder. Trying to emotionally overpower her or gain control will get you nowhere, but steadiness and clarity will see you through. Just remember: a boundary is not to be used as a threat—not ever—it is simply part of a broader structure that you give, as a gift, to your family. When you hold to it with quiet strength, you communicate not only your *expectations* but also your *reliability*. But to do this, you must approach it from a place of absolute emotional calm. You need to be completely stable and in control of yourself. If need be, focus on your breathing and strong posture to help you maintain your equilibrium. When done properly, boundaries don't create distance—they increase safety and connection. When done wrong, from fear, anger, or insecurity, however, a woman feels coerced, trapped, and deeply unsafe. Fortunately, deep down, she wants boundaries. She wants to know where she stands. Where you stand. Which, ultimately, is between her and the big, bad world. That's why her trust in you and your ability to enforce reasonable boundaries will make her feel more secure and more loving, not less.

The Role of Consequences

As mentioned, her initial reaction to boundaries will almost always be *resistance* and *rejection*. That's normal. No one likes rules or limits at first. But if you hold firm in a healthy way, *that resistance will eventually turn into relief*. Again, it's a lot like parenting. If you set a bedtime for your kids, they won't immediately comply. They'll test you, ask for water, sneak out of bed, or push back. Only through consistency will they realize that the rule is real and gain the health and the calm that this structure provides. The same applies to adult relationships. A boundary isn't real until it's tested. If she pushes back, it's not necessarily disrespect—it's often just her trying to see if you really meant it.

In order to show that your structures are safe and your boundaries are fair, you need to ensure that the consequences you enact are proportionate and reasonable. If you do something disproportionate or unreasonable—like cancelling her credit card because she swore at you—she won't learn anything from it. At least, nothing positive. She'll learn that you are unpredictable, unsafe, and emotionally weak. So, too, if you set a boundary just to prove that you can't be pushed around, to assert power, or to punish her, she will sense it. Unreasonable consequences—like financial control, threats to leave, or unreasonable ultimatums—are tyrannical and will only create more conflict and fear. A boundary needs to reinforce respect, not fear. Women are incredibly intuitive about emotional intent. As such, if she perceives that your boundary is about control rather than love, it will create more pain and instability and will damage the relationship.

For this reason, you need to be absolutely clear in your own mind that the boundary is being set for the sake of the relationship's well-being while keeping in mind that without enforcement, boundaries are meaningless. For example, if she continues bringing friends home late at night despite your boundary, a reasonable consequence might be calmly insisting that they leave, no matter how poorly received this might be by the late-night guests. Or the next day, if she asks to watch a show together, you might say, "No, I'd rather watch it alone. I didn't like what happened last night." It's not about punishing—it's about showing, through action, that boundaries matter and that your consequences are fair. When you communicate it from a place of love and wisdom, she will feel the difference. If, however, she detects even a hint of the tyrannical king—an attempt to "put her in her place"—she will reject it outright. With that in mind, it's worth remembering a modified version of the golden rule: do not impose consequences on another that you would not wish to have imposed on you.

That said, there must be some consequences. Just as unclear rules and a lack of accountability creates chaos in a workplace, inconsistent boundaries and no accountability creates instability in a relationship. If certain behaviors are tolerated sometimes but punished at other times, it leads to chaos, confusion, and insecurity. A lack of consistency makes her unsure of where she stands, which only breeds resentment and further conflict. To lead well, you must be clear, consistent, and fair in enforcing boundaries. But just as important, the consequences must also be reasonable. If she forgets to do the dishes one night, a reasonable response is discussing it and adjusting expectations—not making an extreme threat like selling her car or refusing to put the kids to bed for a month. Over-the-top reactions reveal insecurity and an attempt to dominate rather than lead. This is the Tyrannical King she fears not the Wise King she respects—and desires.

But perhaps you're not even sure how to set a boundary in the first place. Obviously, there's going to be more than one way, but a good place to begin is stating the need. For example, "I need you to not bring friends home late at night." Then you can add some context by describing the problematic behavior: "Last night, you said you'd be home at midnight but you brought home four friends, which woke me up." Follow this up by explaining the impact this had. You might say, "This affects my sleep, makes me grumpy with the kids, and causes resentment." But instead of leaving it there, offer some constructive alternatives. You could ask, "What do you need instead? Would it help to meet them earlier in the day or for lunch instead of dinner?" This approach—1. stating the need, 2. describing the behavior, 3. explaining the impact, and 4. offering alternatives—enables you to establish boundaries in a clear, personal, and solution-oriented way, while avoiding the pitfalls of being a tyrant. Expect to spend some time in negotiation with the fourth step—my strong recommendation is to keep negotiating until *both* of you are happy with the decision. Over time, this consistency shows her that you mean what you say. She will feel safer—not because she is being controlled, but because she is with a man who has self-mastery, integrity, and a clear vision for the relationship.

Is She Ready?

As with many things in marriage, there is a time for making boundaries and a time for holding fire. As it's often said, there's a season for everything. Before setting boundaries, both you and your partner need to be ready. For her, a good checklist will mirror most of the things we've covered in this book—beginning with trust. More specifically, have you restored it? Does she trust you right now? Is she confident that you understand what went wrong in the relationship? Does she know that you truly grasp why she pulled away, why she lost connection, or why she became disinterested? Likewise, does she feel that you have the ability to listen carefully and will validate her feelings—even if the specific issue she brings up (e.g., the dishes, a late text, a forgotten plan) seems small, because, as you know, it often represents something deeper. Lastly, has she climbed a few rungs on the trust ladder? In short, has safety and connection returned to the relationship? If so, you can check that box.

This should also seem like old news, but the checklist includes her feeling safe, which includes feeling seen, special, and supported. If she's feeling like her emotions and experiences are acknowledged and understood, you know she's being seen. If her burdens are shared and her needs are met, then she's feeling supported. And if she's cherished, appreciated, and valued above all other women, she'll feel special too. On top of that, she needs to feel physically safe as well, otherwise she won't be emotionally safe and secure either—so make sure that you've ticked these boxes as well. Not just once, but continually and for some time. If you have, then well done. If not, neither of you is ready for boundary making.

Next up, is that you've gained her respect. This is essential, because it's not enough to be emotionally present with her. She also needs to respect you, otherwise she won't be respectful of your boundaries. If you try to enforce a boundary without her respecting you, it will come across as insecure and demanding, not as leadership. That's why you need to ensure that you've been honoring your commitments—in both word and deed—doing everything you've said you'd do. But it's not just that. You need to make sure that you've been taking the initiative, both in your own life, as well as in your relationship. This includes anticipating what needs to be done and doing it without waiting for her instructions—be it the dishes or financial matters. And to do all of this you need to have self-discipline. Without that, you won't have her respect. She'll be measuring how you manage your health, work, and personal growth, and her respect will grow accordingly. But the main takeaway here is that respect has to be earned. It can't be asked for. Don't seek her approval, win it. Don't hesitate, act. Don't avoid responsibility, own it. Do that, and you'll get all the respect you deserve, as well as enough respect to move down the list.

An important disclaimer: if you're reading this in order to ensure you never get to a divorce, and your relationship is in a good place, you can start with boundaries today; but, if your wife is feeling unsafe, unsupported, and unloved, with one foot already out the door, boundaries out-of-nowhere will cause the other foot to follow. There must be a foundation of trust and respect before you have any reasonable hope of these boundaries being respected in the relationship.

The next item is pretty obvious, but it's worth mentioning. You need to ensure that her Love Switch is turned on and her Mood Glasses aren't dark. As you know by now, when a woman's feeling emotionally disconnected, she will only perceive facts that confirm her current emotional state. If she is frustrated, she will focus on past frustrations and dismiss all the good things you have done. Likewise, if you try to set a boundary while she is in a negative emotional state, she will react negatively. She will interpret it as control, not leadership. The key is to wait until her Love Switch is on at least *somewhat* consistently and her mood is positive—when she is engaged, affectionate, and open. If you can't tell whether that's the case, now is not the time to try. Instead, go back to the chapter on the Love Switch and Mood Glasses and read up, because you've still got work to do.

In essence, the entire checklist boils down to this: that she feels safe with you, trusts you, and respects you. If she does, it's the right time to set boundaries. But given that you don't want to get the timing wrong, you can assess her readiness by checking for the following signs.

1. Emotional Appreciation—She starts showing gratitude, even subtly (e.g., making you a snack, doing something thoughtful).
2. Physical Affection—She initiates touch more often—holding hands, sitting close, resting her head on you.
3. Initiating Time Together—She invites you to spend time together, whether it's watching a movie or running errands.
4. Verbal Affirmation—She makes small positive comments about things you do, even if she isn't outright saying "thank you" yet.

5. Sharing More About Her Life—She starts opening up about work, friendships, or personal struggles, showing deeper emotional trust.
6. Talking Positively About the Future—Instead of avoiding future plans, she casually mentions vacations, shared goals, or long-term ideas.
7. Initiating Intimacy—A strong sign of emotional connection is when she initiates intimacy rather than just responding to it.
8. Explicit Verbal Appreciation—If she directly says, "I appreciate what you've been doing," it means she deeply trusts the new dynamic.
9. Deferring to Your Leadership—Instead of criticizing or instructing, she starts asking for your opinion and guidance.

Again—this is a checklist for men whose wives are already considering leaving. If the relationship is barely holding on boundaries at the wrong time could break it. You need to reestablish trust before the boundaries will work. But if you are already at a good place in your marriage—or are starting a new relationship—the sooner you begin to set boundaries the better. This minimizes the likelihood of needing to repair the relationship later in order to be able to set boundaries again. So, if you can detect most of these signs, not just once but on a regular basis, then you're absolutely ready. These signs indicate that she feels emotionally connected to you and your boundaries will not only *work* but they will massively increase the trust and connection in the relationship.

Are You Ready?

It's not enough that a woman feels ready for boundaries. You need to feel ready too. The worst thing you can do is go into this fainthearted, because inconsistency or timidity will undo all your efforts. It will put you further back than you were before. To that end, you need to ensure that you're ready, from top to bottom, both inside and out. Like her checklist, you must reach a number of personal milestones before setting them up. If you've reached these, you should have all the confidence and clarity you need to set effective, reasonable and respected boundaries.

The first milestone is that you've taken full ownership of your relationship's past mistakes. That's not the same as taking all the blame. But it is you making 'the mistakes' *your* business. Your responsibility. That means no scapegoating. No compartmentalizing. You need to own what has gone wrong in the relationship, whether it was baggage from a past breakup, trauma from your earlier life, or an ongoing dynamic that has not been working. This is necessary, because if she does not believe you fully understand why she pulled away, why she was upset, or why she lost respect for you, she will not trust that anything has truly changed. To do this, you must be able to acknowledge past mistakes without being defensive or dismissive. You need to clearly communicate to her that you understand her emotions, not just the surface complaints but the deeper reasons behind them. Furthermore, you must demonstrate real change, not just in words but through consistent actions that show you have internalized what she needed from you.

A second milestone is that you've maintained at least several weeks of consistently strong behavior. As in *you*, not *her*. You need to be able to look back over the last few weeks or months and confidently say that you have handled yourself well. You should be able to recognize that you have not had emotional outbursts or impatience, nor have you engaged in passive-aggressive or retaliatory behavior. More importantly, you should feel proud of how you have conducted yourself as a partner. This period of consistency is crucial because it proves to both you and her that your changes are not temporary or performative. If you have spent long enough responding with patience, emotional maturity, and stability, then you are in a strong place to introduce boundaries with confidence. However, if you still find yourself having emotional blowups, losing patience, or acting from frustration, it is a sign that more internal work is needed before setting boundaries, because right now *you aren't even following your own*. And if emotional regulation is a persistent issue, consider joining a coaching program, like mine, that can help you overcome this.

Next, you need to have confidence in yourself. In your own worth. This should come fairly naturally after you've seen a few months of genuine self-improvement. You might notice around this time that you've stopped second-guessing yourself because you know you have done the right things. As a result, you no longer feel the need to prove yourself, as your actions now speak for themselves. More importantly, you begin to recognize that you *deserve* respect and appreciation. At this stage, if she continues to treat you with disrespect or disregard, you no longer feel confused about whether you have done something wrong. Instead, you recognize that the imbalance is on *her*, not on *you*. This is the moment where you can confidently say to yourself, "I have done the work, I have been a good man, and if I am still not being respected, *this is not my failure.*" This is a momentous moment as a man. Instead of worrying about whether you are the problem, you can see clearly that you have done *everything in your power* to build a healthy dynamic. If she does not appreciate that, the issue lies with her, not with you. You no longer have to wonder, from a place of insecurity and confusion, about the problem. You can have, maybe for the first time, total confidence and clarity that *you are a good man* and her unwillingness to recognize that is *not on you*. Now, that's not to say that you should call it quits just because you've been on your best behavior for two weeks or two months and she hasn't. That's missing the point. Rather, it's as you witness the positive changes in yourself—as you come to know that they're both real and lasting—you mustn't allow her negativity to define you and your understanding of the relationship.

This is linked to the last milestone, which is overcoming your fear. Namely, the fear that boundaries will cause tension, distance, or even the end of the relationship. For some, this prevents them from erecting any boundaries at all. For others, it undermines even their best efforts—because if fear drives your boundary-setting, it will come across in your conduct. She will sense it. She will pick up on uncertainty in your voice, hesitation in your stance, and the underlying fear that she might leave if you stand your ground. And when a woman senses this fear, she will not respect the boundary. Instead, she will test it even harder to see if you actually mean it—very possibly test it to the point where you break, give in, and reaffirm to her that your boundaries are not, in fact, real. A boundary is only respected when it is delivered from a place of unwavering, calm confidence, not from insecurity or desperation. The good news is that when you reach this milestone of personal growth, setting boundaries becomes effortless because you are no longer afraid of the fall-out. You are no longer asking yourself, "What if she doesn't like this?" Instead, you are thinking, "This is what I deserve, and I won't accept less."

In fact, once you have reached this milestone, the way you set boundaries will naturally change. Instead of saying, "Hey, I really need you to stop speaking to me that way," in a hesitant, approval-seeking tone, you will simply state, "I don't allow people to speak to me like that," in a firm, matter-of-fact manner. You will actually *mean it*. And she will recognize that. This delivery will increase the likelihood of her respecting the boundary tenfold. Also from this place, instead of fearing what will happen if she reacts negatively, you will recognize that if she respects you, she will honor the boundary. If she does not, that is a sign of a deeper issue.

Though the number of your milestones is less than the length of her checklist, you need to make sure that you've reached them all. This means:

1. That you've taken full ownership of past mistakes—demonstrating real change.
2. That you've had at least several weeks (ideally a few months) of consistent, stable, and mature behavior.
3. That you've got confidence in your actions and self-worth—you know you deserve respect.
4. That you're free from fear—you are not afraid of losing the relationship if your boundaries are not respected.

This last milestone is the most liberating and important of all, because it comes with the empowering realization that *you do not need to stay in a marriage where you are not respected.* You *may want to stay* for a variety of reasons and I applaud your commitment—in many ways, therein lies the difference between dating and a marriage. Marriages, unlike mere relationships, are premised on the promise that you'll stick it out, for better or for worse. That you'll have stamina. Courage. Resolve. But—and this is a major but—you do not have to stay aboard a sinking ship. Not if you've made every effort to keep it afloat. Not if you've done your duty. You've manned your post. Granted, a few weeks of genuine, even massive effort doesn't represent your all. I've had many, many clients who stuck it out in this rebuilding phase for a year or more, experiencing only pain all the while, and being rewarded with the marriage of their dreams as a result after 12 or 15 months. I am a massive advocate not only of marriage but of being willing to suffer for what matters most. But there does come a time when it's okay to abandon ship. When you can get in the life raft and say, with a pure heart, I did *everything* I could. *That doesn't mean you have to*, but at least you can see now that you've got a choice. That it's your choice, not hers. Because, now, finally, you are a Sovereign Man. You are the King of your own Kingdom. You, my friend, are a slave to no one.

To Conclude

The flood is real. I know that. You know that. She knows that. You can't avoid it and in actual fact, you shouldn't. Instead, you should take on the mantle, the burden, of leadership. Meet the flood—and meet her—with stability, security, care, and strength. But do so in order to *support* the river, not to *control* it. To honor the river's beauty and energy, not because you're intimidated by its intensity. To that end, as you seek to create positive Masculine Structure, don't be afraid to develop certainty about yourself. Have courage in setting reasonable boundaries. Act with vision and direction. Be the floodgate, the rock, The Lighthouse. Lead through service, earning her trust and cooperation rather than demanding it. In short, don't be a coward or act like a tyrant. Be the Wise King, creating safety, not distance; setting boundaries in strength, not from fear; and enforcing them with love, not as a means of control. In time, not only will the queen thank you, but you'll thank yourself—and in the end, as much as a happy wife makes a happy life, it is your own self-respect that is the determining factor of your ultimate fulfillment in life.

A Man's Work

You're nearly there. These last two exercises help you define what you stand for and become the man who enforces it with calm, not control. Don't wait for chaos to draw the line. Know it, name it, live it. That's how a King leads with strength and love.

1) Boundary Clarity Journal (Journaling Prompt)

Instructions: Set boundaries with love. Identify one recurring issue (e.g., harsh tone). Write in your notebook a four-part plan: 1) The boundary, 2) Why it matters, 3) A consequence, 4) A better way. Next, write down your answers to the following questions: What fears do I have? How would enforcing this help us? Reread this later in the week to check your progress and help you to hold your ground.

Purpose: This clarifies and prepares you to set (and stick to) fair boundaries.

2) Avatar: Who You Could Be

Instructions: Similar to our previous avatar exercise, design your strongest self yet—the man who sets boundaries with calm clarity. Give him a dramatic name (even if it feels cheesy). Describe how he moves, speaks, leads in conflict. Now be him: 1) Speak as him in the mirror. 2) Talk on the phone as him. 3) Be him at work. 4) Choose a boundary today and uphold it. Remember, this isn't about acting—it's about actually becoming the King she trusts and desires.

Purpose: This is an essential aspect of crowning the King, because no kingdom can exist without boundaries.

Notes to Self

CONCLUSION

Long Live The King

Here we are. The end of one road, the start of another. If you've made it this far, you've walked through the muck of your own soul, stared down the Storms of your marriage, and begun to forge something stronger—both in yourself and in the life you share with your wife. This book wasn't meant to be a quick fix or a feel-good pat on the back. It's been a gauntlet, a call to arms, a map to reclaim what's been lost: your sovereignty, your marriage, your kingdom. And now, as the dust settles and the final pages turn, it's time to ask—what does it all mean? Where do you go from here? How do you take these nine laws and turn them into a life worth living?

Let's rewind for a moment. Back to the beginning, where I laid it out plain: we're in a masculinity crisis. You felt it before you picked up this book—that gnawing sense that something's off, that men aren't what they used to be, or at least not what they should be. Maybe it hit you in the quiet of a lonely night, staring at divorce papers you never thought you'd see. Maybe it was the slow drift of a marriage growing cold, the kids asking why Mommy and Daddy don't laugh anymore. Or maybe it was subtler—a vague unease, a whisper that you're not really... a MAN... not like you thought you'd be by this stage of life. Whatever brought you here, you're not alone. I've been there too—sprawled out, drunk, wondering how my life went from chaos to collapse, only to find my anchor in the faces of my kids and a determination that my family would not be broken.

That's where this started for me, and maybe where it started for you too—a moment of reckoning. But here's the truth we've uncovered together: the wreckage isn't the end. It's the beginning. The crisis isn't a death sentence; it's an invitation. And these nine laws? They're not just rules or a checklist to save your marriage—they're a blueprint to reclaim your crown, to step into your power as a Sovereign Man. Because a King doesn't just rule his castle; he builds it, brick by brick, with sweat, grit, and a heart wide open.

The Journey From Slave to Sovereign

It all begins with the first law: *master yourself.* You can't lead a kingdom if you're still bowing to shadows—booze, porn, anger, avoidance, the endless scroll of escape. I've seen it in my own life and in the men I coach: broken men break things. Whole men heal them. That's why we started with the hard truth—you've got to break free from the chains you've forged, whether they're wrapped around your wrists or your heart. You've mapped your chains, faced your winter, and envisioned your Inner King. Maybe you've even taken that first step, choosing sovereignty over slavery in a heated moment with your wife. It's not easy. It's raw, painful, and humbling. But it's the only way to stand tall as The Lighthouse she needs when her Storms roll in.

And those Storms *will* roll in. That's why the second law is the injunction to *be The Lighthouse.* Remember, she's not testing you with her Storm because she hates you; she's testing you because she needs you. When she hurls her fears and insecurities your way, it's not about winning an argument—it's about proving you're bigger than the chaos. I've stood in Whitney's Storms and learned the hard way that storming back gets you nowhere. But standing steady and unfazed? That's when she softens, when she finds her calm in your presence. It's not about logic or fixing her feelings; it's about being the rock she can depend on. You've got the breathwork now, the posture, the patience. Use it.

Then came the third law: *do not take the factbait.* Men see facts; women feel feelings. You've dodged the bait by now, haven't you? That moment when she's ranting about the dishes or the dog, and you resist the urge to list your chore stats. Good. Because it's not about the dishes—it's about her heart. Meet her there, and you'll bridge the divide. Laws four and five—*flip the Love Switch* and *lighten her Mood Glasses*—doubled down on this. Her love can flip off and on like a bulb, her world tinted dark or rosy by the moment. Don't panic when it's off. Don't take her words as gospel when the glasses are dim. Lift her spirits—joke with her, take her out, give her a break—and watch the switch flip, the lenses clear. I've picked Whitney up and spun her around in a dark mood and seen her laugh through tears. You can too.

Law six hit harder: *no fear*. This one's a gut-punch. You're not just her husband—you're the bear in the room. Your anger, your edge, it's not passion when directed at her; it's a threat. I've picked a lock to "resolve" an argument, only to see terror in Whitney's eyes. Never again. You've learned to calm the bear, to step away, to ask if she's afraid. It's not weakness—it's strength. And law seven builds on that: *she needs to feel seen, special, and supported*. Safety isn't just physical; it's emotional. She needs to know you see her fears, cherish her uniqueness, and have her back. Send her to the bedroom with wine and a show. Plan a date she doesn't have to think about. Watch her soften, her feminine core shine. That's your superpower.

Law eight, *building trust*, took us to a higher place. Trust isn't a gift; it's a ladder climbed step by step, tested by her Storms. You've passed a test or two by now—stayed calm when she pushed, held firm when she provoked. It's brutal, but it's a victory. She's not crazy; she's verifying. And when you stand unshaken, she climbs higher, her gratitude delayed but real. Finally, the ninth law: *establish boundaries*. You're the bank to her river, not the dam. You've set lines—firm, fair, loving—and held them with quiet strength. She resists, then relaxes. The flood calms, and your kingdom thrives.

The Payoff: A Kingdom Restored

So, what's the payoff? Why endure this gauntlet? Picture this: a marriage where she looks at you with love and adoration in her eyes, not because you've groveled, but because you've earned it through strength and love. A home where the kids see a King and Queen, not an asshole and a 'crazy ex-wife' in the making. A life where you wake up proud, not haunted. That's what these laws build—not just a patched-up relationship, but a kingdom restored. I've seen it in my own life. Whitney and I went from separate beds and separate cities to a marriage that's raw, real, and alive. I've watched clients—men with divorce papers in hand—turn it around, not by begging, but by becoming Sovereign. You can too.

It's not magic. It's not a fairy tale. It's work—relentless, unglamorous, soul-deep work. You've got the tools now: the breathwork to steady you, the journaling to unearth you, the actions to prove you. You've mapped your chains, faced your past, and crowned your King. You've stood as The Lighthouse, dodged the factbait, flipped the switch, and held the line. But the payoff isn't just her softening—it's you. The man you become through this isn't just a better husband; he's a better man. Stronger. Steadier. Sovereign.

The Road Ahead: Living the Laws

This isn't the end—it's the beginning. These nine laws aren't a one-and-done deal; they're a way of life. You'll stumble. You'll fail. There'll be days when the slave whispers louder than the King, when her Storm feels like a tsunami, when the boundary you set gets trampled. That's okay. Kings don't win every battle—they win the war. Get back up. Breathe. Reflect. Act. Each law is a thread in the tapestry of your sovereignty, and every time you weave them into your days, the fabric gets stronger.

Start small. Master yourself in the quiet moments—five minutes of breathwork before the day begins, a journal entry naming one chain you'll break today. Be The Lighthouse when she's grumpy over breakfast, not just when she's screaming over dinner. Dodge the factbait in a text spat, not just a blowout. Flip her switch with a goofy grin, not a grand gesture. Check her safety when your voice rises, even slightly. Make her feel seen with a question, special with a compliment, supported with a chore done unasked.

Build trust rung by rung—listen to her grocery store saga, not just her trauma. Set a boundary over something trivial—screen time, not infidelity—and hold it with love. Small wins stack up. They become habits. Habits become character. Character becomes a kingdom.

And don't do it alone. Find men who get it—friends, a coach, a group. I sold my finance business and built a life coaching men because I saw the hunger, the ache, in guys like you. Reach out (@the_sovereign_man) if you need a guide. Iron sharpens iron. You're not meant to climb this ladder in isolation.

The Stakes: It's Not Just About You Two

It's easy to forget about others, but the stakes are higher than your marriage. Your wife's not the only one watching—your kids are too. Your coworkers. Your neighbors. The world. A man who masters himself and his marriage doesn't just heal his home; he heals the culture. We're drowning in noise—political shouting matches, economic rollercoasters, a society that celebrates weakness over strength. Families are fracturing, trust is evaporating, and masculinity's either mocked or misunderstood. You're the antidote. One Sovereign Man at a time, one marriage at a time, we turn the tide. You lift your wife, your kids, your community. Every healed man, leading his family from a place of strength and love, creates a ripple effect with no predetermined end.

I think of my own kids. Thanks to the progress we've made they didn't just see us survive—they saw us thrive. They saw a King step up, not a slave crumble. That's what you're building for your kids too, if you have them now or in the future—a legacy of strength, not surrender. And for your wife? She gets the man she dreamed of, not the shadow she settled for. She gets to shine as the queen she is, not drown in a flood she can't contain.

The Final Charge: Crown Yourself

So, here's my final charge to you: crown yourself. Not with arrogance or tyranny, but with the quiet, steady resolve of a man who knows who he is and why he's here. You've got the laws. You've got the work. You've got the vision. Step into it. The King within you isn't a fantasy—he's real, waiting to rise. Every time you choose him over the slave, you forge that crown in the fire of your own will. It's heavy, sure. It's not for the faint-hearted. But it's yours.

Long live the King—not just in these pages, but in your life. In your marriage. In your kingdom. You've got this. I've seen it happen—men who couldn't look me in the eye on day one walking out six weeks later like they own the room. Their wives saw it first: a softer tone, a firmer boundary, a presence that wasn't there before. You'll see it too. She'll feel it. Your world will change. Not because you forced it, but because you earned it.

When the King heals himself, the kingdom heals itself. When the King finds his strength, the kingdom finds its strength. It is my sincere hope that this book has helped guide you in this process of healing yourself, finding your strength, and ascending to the throne. Good luck, King.

Notes to Self

Want More Support?

If you found this helpful and you think you could benefit from additional help, know this: **This book represents only about 2% of what's inside my full coaching programs.**

Inside the Sovereign Man Mastermind, I walk you step by step, stage by stage, through exactly how to save your marriage from the brink of divorce—and how to make it divorce-proof for life.

The coursework is built on my **Archetypal Integration and Depth Coaching (AIDC)** system: the most comprehensive and practical masculine transformation program in the world. It's designed to help you reclaim your confidence, emotional power, leadership, and clarity as a man.

We offer:

- Free courses for men just starting out

- Group programs with daily coaching calls

- Private 1-on-1 mentorship with me or my top coaches

- Lifetime-access coursework that evolves as you do

- Whatever level of support you need—we've got you

If you think you could benefit from additional help to save what matters most to you... then you owe it to yourself to go to www.divorceproofman.com and commit to the future you demand.

APPENDIX 1

Here are eight sequential, self-reflective tasks designed to progressively guide you from a state of emotional, mental, and spiritual slavery toward sovereignty. These tasks build intentionally upon each other, aligned with the core principles of mastering oneself in order to master marriage and life.

Task 1: Mapping Your Kingdom

Objective: Identify clearly and honestly the current state of your life and the areas in which you're enslaved.

Exercise:

• Write out an honest inventory of the forces currently controlling your life:

　• Addictions or harmful habits (alcohol, porn, gambling, food).

　• Emotional dependencies (approval-seeking, fear of rejection, anxiety).

　• Avoidance behaviors (withdrawing, emotional checking-out, escapism).

　• Identify the single strongest chain holding you back today.

　• Journal about the consequences these forces have had on your marriage, family, career, and self-worth.

Task 2: Excavating the Past

Objective: Understand how past wounds, traumas, or experiences feed into your current enslavement.

Exercise:

• Describe in detail one significant childhood experience or trauma that still influences your behavior today.

• Journal on how this unresolved issue specifically impacts your reactions, habits, or patterns in marriage and self-leadership.

• Complete the sentence: "I am still enslaved by this experience because..."

Task 3: Facing the Winter

Objective: Confront your deepest emotional pain, acknowledging what you must let go in order to change.

Exercise:

• Write about your personal "winter": the emptiness or pain you feel most intensely right now.

• Clearly identify and articulate three harmful patterns or beliefs that must be discarded for you to move forward.

• Commit to one concrete action step you will take today toward releasing these patterns, even if it is uncomfortable.

Task 4: Envisioning Your Inner King

Objective: Begin to conceptualize your Higher Self—your Sovereign, inner King.

Exercise:

• Write a vivid description of your Higher Self: how he speaks, moves, acts, thinks, and reacts.

• Imagine three challenging scenarios (a conflict with your wife, a moment of temptation, an urge to escape), and write exactly how your Inner King would handle each situation differently than your current self.

End by clearly stating why you want to become this Higher Self.

Task 5: Choosing Sovereignty

Objective: Practice consciously choosing sovereignty over slavery in real-time situations.

Exercise:

• Throughout today, pause at three critical moments when you feel tempted to slip into old habits.

• Each time, journal briefly:

  • What were you feeling?

  • What did you nearly choose?

  • What choice would your Higher Self make?

  • Which choice did you actually make?

End by reflecting on what you learned from this real-time exercise in sovereignty.

Task 6: Claiming Responsibility

Objective: Take ownership of the damage done by past abdications of sovereignty.

Exercise:

• Write a letter (you don't have to send it yet) to your wife clearly taking responsibility for specific harm you've caused through your previous emotional or behavioral slavery.

• Explicitly describe the changes you're committed to making.

• After completing the letter, journal about the emotions that arise—fear, shame, relief, resolve—and what they tell you about your current state.

Task 7: Building a Bridge

Objective: Rebuild trust and connection by demonstrating consistent growth.

Exercise:

• For seven consecutive days, intentionally perform one tangible, sovereign action that actively rebuilds trust with your wife (e.g., a sincere apology, patience during a disagreement, presence instead of withdrawal).

• After each action, journal briefly on how you felt and your wife's response or reaction.

• Reflect at week's end on the patterns you notice and the ways in which your marriage is subtly shifting because of your commitment to change.

Task 8: Crown the King

Objective: Solidify your new identity by formally stepping into sovereignty.

Exercise:

• Compose a formal written oath or personal creed that clearly outlines who you now choose to be as a man, husband, and leader.

• Include specific promises about how you'll act differently, how you'll maintain sovereignty, and the habits or values you will uphold moving forward.

• Share this creed verbally with someone you deeply trust (ideally your wife) as a symbolic act of publicly committing to your new identity.

• Journal afterward about how this commitment feels and the vision you now hold for your future kingdom.

APPENDIX II
NOTES

Divorce-Proof Man

www.ingramcontent.com/pod-product-compliance
Lightning Source LLC
Chambersburg PA
CBHW020340010526
44119CB00048B/548